Food for Thought Truck

How a San Francisco design
firm turned an ice cream
truck into a mobile studio
and took it on the road in
pursuit of new perspectives.

Thank You

A project as far ranging as Food for Thought Truck is the work of many
people. Our team would like to thank all those who contributed time
and talent to this effort. Special thanks to Phil Horton and Doyle
Buddington for turning a design into a truck and to our many partners
in the field for making every stop an adventure: in San Jose and
Fremont, Marie Millares, Kevin Biggers, Isaiah Wilson; in Bakersfield,
Daniel and Monica Cater, David Coffey, Shai and Stasie Bitton, Andrae
Gonzales, Ash Dipert and the people of Eastchester; in Los Angeles,
Jason Foster, Brandon Tate, Angela Barranco and all those who posted
signs declaring their proximity to the Los Angeles River.

Thanks to those in our O+A family who contributed their enthusiasm and
100% commitment despite setbacks, detours, nights far from home and a
vehicle that shook like a roller coaster.

Verda Alexander
Alex Bautista
Lisa Bieringer
Melanie Brignone
Marbel Calderon
Emily Cano
Kristina Cho
George Craigmyle
Stefani Ferreira
Javier Gallardo
Kayla Goldberg
Michael Griffin
Nikki Hall
Lauren Harrison
Sean Houghton
Alexis Kraft
Liliana Lewicka
Chase Lunt
Paulina McFarland
Al McKee
Rachelle Meneses
Keyairra Murray
Primo Orpilla
Kaylen Parker
Alex Pokas
Lauren Perich
Joseph Rodriguez
Aditi Saldanha
Elizabeth Vereker
Mindi Weichman
Amy Young

STUDIO O+A

452 Tehama Street
San Francisco, CA 94103

PUBLISHER

Artifice Press
81 Rivington Street
London EC2A 3AY

The Kickoff

Why a food truck?
Verda gets ahead of herself.
Interior design as a moral profession.
Marbel tells a story.

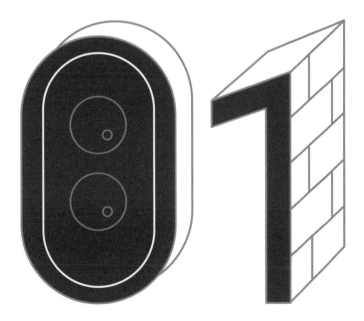

6

NOVEMBER 2017

"Oh God!"

Verda Alexander's groan is part of the culture at O+A. All the designers know it well. It is her way of signaling that a meeting has gone on too long and her expression of solidarity with a fellow designer's travails. It is her standard answer to the question, "How did it go?" after a client presentation or an art exhibition or a trip to China. Today, on the eve of the Food for Thought Truck kickoff, it is a song of new project angst. "Sometimes I think it's going to be amazing," she says. "It's going to be this really crazy, creative endeavor, and other times..." —here, laughter begins to fray her words— "...other times I think it's the stupidest idea in the world!" She allows herself a few seconds of levity at the thought of a project to which she has committed the full resources of her company turning out to be a crackpot scheme. Then she quickly composes herself and sits up straight. "No. I'm excited."

This is the feeling every designer experiences at the launch of a new effort. Will it work out okay? Will my design sense come through or will it fail me? Will I know that it's failed me? An interior design project is such a complex and expensive undertaking, involving so many elements and so many people—most of them highly opinionated about what is or isn't possible, is or isn't cool —that presenting a design proposal is like auditioning for a Broadway show. Everyone sits there looking at you with a poker face while you go through your humble paces. No wonder the start of every project is an occasion for angst.

Today, at least, the poker faces belong, not to clients, but to other members of the team. Verda walks into a conference room full of people she has hand-picked for the project—people she has worked with successfully in the past, but also people with a particular and relevant expertise. Chase Lunt knows something about auto mechanics. Kristina Cho writes and photographs a food blog. Eight faces in all have gathered around the table, not counting Verda (or Primo Orpilla, her

At the outset every project is limitlessly inventive, brave and impactful. Then the work begins.

co-founder at O+A)—a pretty large team for a project the size of an ice cream truck.

"I want to start with a quote I read in an article about Thomas Edison," Verda says. She reads from a handwritten note: "'Deliberate experimentation is more important than deliberate practice in a rapidly changing world.'" She's referring to an article by Michael Simmons on the online writers' forum medium. com. Simmons refutes Malcolm Gladwell's popular assertion that 10,000 hours of practice is the road to expertise in any field, arguing that, in periods of rapid change, experimentation is a surer path to success than practice. It's an idea that appeals to Verda's preference for not repeating yourself, for tackling every project as if it's your first. "I think that a lot of what we do here is deliberate practice," she says now to the Food for Thought Truck team. "I want to set the bar for doing things differently. It's definitely going to be more of an artistic process, more a process of flying by the seat of our pants. This particular project is going to be about experimentation and our willingness to fail. And it's kind of a bummer, but it's going to be a crazy fast schedule."

She turns to Lisa Bieringer, the principal at O+A currently in charge of keeping the firm in the black. Lisa reads through the breakneck schedule for this project: truck purchased and in hand by end of November; design development done by January; fabricators chosen and construction drawings finished in February; construction wrapped up by the end of April...

"We want to have the truck on the road by May 15th," Verda says.

She stops. All around the table: attentive faces —and not a glimmer of comprehension.

"Do you all know the plan?" she says. "Do you know the brief?"

The room explodes in laughter. With Thomas Edison-style alacrity, Verda has plunged into the particulars of the project before explaining what the project is.

"Okay, okay," she laughs. "Let's back up."

– – –

In 2015 O+A sent a team to the London Design Festival with the intention of uncorking West Coast workplace thinking in the middle of buttoned-up Holborn. Verda's idea for the installation was to turn a food truck into a mobile co-working space,

park it on the street in Central London and invite people to come inside and work. The project blended radical workplace design—shifting functions, shared amenities—with classic American road culture, and it perfectly expressed the O+A spirit, then at high tide, of questioning all the old conventions of workplace.

In the end, transferring a truck from California to England—or buying one and fitting it out in the UK—proved too logistically complicated for the time allowed, and O+A's West Coast East exhibit at the LDF turned into a more modest installation. But Verda never let go of her idea and when in 2017 the opportunity arose to document an O+A project in a book—which became this book—the food truck office seemed ideal. There was no client to keep happy, no fees at stake, no commercial considerations. True, in the four years since Verda conceived the idea, mobile offices had become as common as Starbucks, but that only required adjusting the concept. The central elements—mobility, spatial limitations, new approaches to work, new applications for design—remained evergreen.

The revised concept that Verda is presenting today is a variation on that original idea: a mobile design lab. "O+A on wheels," she calls it, although not the O+A that has worked out of stationary offices in the Bay Area for a quarter-century. This food truck version will travel around the state doling out design like an architectural taco truck. It will be an experimental studio committed to more audacious, less commercial projects than the firm has undertaken for profit, and at the same time a community outreach program that will bring first-rate design to places where it hasn't been much valued—to underfunded schools, perhaps, or to unlovely corners of unloved neighborhoods. Precisely where, though, isn't clear yet. "One of the things we need to figure out," Verda says, "is what it is that we're going to be doing out there. What design problems are we going to solve? And how are we going to solve them? Are we just going to come up with sketches and ideas and hand them off to someone, or are we going to be out there with hammers and hard hats?"

On the glass walls of the conference room— where the kickoff meeting is now properly underway —the team, per Verda's invitation, have taped up photos of other mobile ventures they find

"We want to have the
truck on the road
by May," Verda says
in November, a goal
that proves unduly
optimistic.

One of the crucial moments
on any design project comes
right at the beginning when
the team determines the
direction of the concept.
It is at this point that
everyone's individual
effort can be sent down
the wrong road toward
something trivial or silly
or quick to grow stale.

F
F
T
T
-
11
-
17

O+A's practice always moves forward with missionary zeal, a belief in design as a vehicle for making things better. You have only to look at the 'before' photos of an O+A project to see how dramatically its work improves the lives of the people who use its spaces. Dark, dim offices with low ceilings and mud-colored carpets, dreary cubicle farms and anonymous hallways, dead-end corners, old water coolers, bulletin boards. This is what O+A rips out, and replaces with… light-drenched, expansive, multi-faceted comfort zones, hip lounge areas, in-house cafés, in-house game rooms, towering wall art, maybe a quiet place to catch a nap, maybe a lemon-yellow staircase. An O+A space really does transform the work experience. Why not then bring that expertise, that power to transform to 'someone who needs it'? Perhaps the Food for Thought Truck will be the vehicle that carries O+A outside its own comfort zone.

⌐ ⌐ ⌐ inspiring. One by one each person gets up and explains a rolling enterprise that sparked his or her interest: a self-driving conference room, a mobile photo studio, a tiny lingerie shop on wheels. Almost all of them are elegantly designed, but is that what Food for Thought Truck wants to be: a stylish architectural gesture?

One of the crucial moments on any design project comes right at the beginning when the team determines the direction of the concept. It is at this point that everyone's individual effort can be sent down the wrong road toward something trivial or silly or quick to grow stale. For that reason it is vitally important that the 'why' of a project be clearly defined and vetted by the firm's toughest critics and why now, as people present their inspirations, Verda resists beautification as a mission for the truck.

Primo has remained largely silent during the meeting. Technically he is a 'guest' today, not officially a designated member of the team, but now he looks up from his laptop. "The why needs to be really compelling," he says. "We're putting our thinking out there—so how do we elevate it? How do we make a connection to someone who needs it? There's an artist called Theaster Gates who took a neighborhood of blight in Chicago, he took old buildings and he created a library, he created areas to listen to music, he tried to create the things this neighborhood never had."

Up to now O+A has not been much involved with 'neighborhoods of blight'. Its clients are mostly venture-funded start-ups and companies already highly successful—tech companies, high profile manufacturers, global brands. But within that niche

As the discussion heats up, with everyone talking at once and ideas flying, the open-ended possibility of doing something important sweeps the room: maybe we could tackle the homeless problem; maybe we could help the Sonoma fire victims; maybe we could work with children. Any time you open your toolbox to the public there is always the possibility of inspiring someone, motivating someone. "You can genuinely have an impact on somebody's life," a fired-up team member says. "If you're introducing them to a career they don't even know exists and they suddenly feel: 'Wow! This is what I want to do.' Years later they'll think back: 'I remember they came in a truck and that was my first introduction to design.'"

From the other end of the table a quiet voice says, "That's how I got into design."

All heads turn. Marbel Calderon has been with O+A for less than a year. A young designer from Orange County, she is part of a wave of new hires that has transformed the staff, made it younger. Now with the confidence of someone who grew her luck from scratch, she shares her story: "So there was a ballet studio in Santa Ana that started in an attic and it was all for low-income families." Marbel and her sister studied at the school, practically lived there she says, while her single mom worked. When the school got funding to build a new facility the architects invited the kids in to see their office. Marbel was nine or ten years old. "I remember one of the architects driving. I was sitting in the front

12

seat and there were two kids in the back and he was telling us all these stories about buildings he had built and I was just amazed." At the office the building models intrigued her, but the revelation was the interiors department with its finish samples and color swatches and 3D renderings pinned to the walls. Even as a kid she knew about architecture, knew that people built buildings, but it had never occurred to her that someone actually designed the inside. "From that day, I knew I was going to be a designer," she says. "It was life-changing."

For a moment the Food for Thought Truck team is silent. Claims of life-changing impact flow through the design world like free champagne, but to have a living demonstration of it sitting right there at your conference table... well, it's like that moment when a designer who has seen his or her work only in renderings steps into the fully constructed space. The transition from idea to reality is always humbling. As conversation resumes around the table, more quietly now, it is weighted with a new understanding that the project O+A is kicking off today really could be momentous, really could be life-changing—or at the very least, not the stupidest idea in the world.

13

The Truck

Searching for a truck online.
Chase and George meet a likely prospect.
Chase sniffs a winner.

Google the phrase 'used food truck' and a multi-colored gallery of automotive ingenuity pops up. Pizza trucks, ice cream trucks, little two- and four-wheel trailers, a converted fire engine, a converted London double-decker bus. Each of these customized mobile kitchens represents someone's dream of independence. And because they are now grouped together in a virtual used truck lot, most are also examples of entrepreneurial dreams gone awry. It's a humbling reminder to those on the team who see this food truck design lab as the prototype for an ongoing enterprise that even dreams built on pizza and ice cream come with no guarantees. Still there's an upside to this gallery of failed businesses: for once the designers will be able to choose their existing conditions.

Most of O+A's projects come to life in existing buildings. It is the base requirement for commercial design, this ability to drop into a vacant cavity of raw concrete and exposed ductwork and turn it into a habitable environment. The hard frame, within which the magic has to happen, often determines what sort of magic is possible. Just as the shape of a stage dictates the shape of the productions that play upon it, the limitations of an existing site are a catalyst to creativity in designing what will go there. It is clear from the outset that a truck will present limitations more severe than any O+A has dealt with before, as well as complications arising from the code—the vehicle code. Still, even a nervous designer must appreciate the logic of this project: to turn the most unlikely of spaces (an old service truck!) into a rolling laboratory that will travel to other unlikely spaces and effect the same metamorphosis there.

To conduct the truck search Verda chooses O+A designer, Chase Lunt. A native of suburban Los Angeles, Chase grew up in a culture in which the car you drove was a major part of your identity. He drove a 1976 Volkswagen van, "the slowest and oldest car" in his high school, but one which established his reputation for free-thinking and

FFTT - 11 - 17

17

Even before a truck is in hand the team is impatient to work with something real.

"It definitely had an
impact, not only on
how I looked at cars,
but on how I looked
at design. Because
it had the flexibility
to do what I wanted
on the inside."

mechanical acumen. "It definitely had an impact, not only on how I looked at cars," he says, "but on how I looked at design. Because it had the flexibility to do what I wanted inside. Unlike modern cars which have a lot of panels and electronics and stuff that just gets in your way, it was a big empty box." Chase still owns his high school VW, and the condition of his copy of *How to Keep Your Volkswagen Alive* is a testament to how central the van has been to his life. Dog-eared, oil-smudged, the pages warped by Lord knows how many rainstorms and puddle-drops, the book suggests a deep familiarity with all things automotive; precisely the familiarity this unique project requires.

Through the month of November, Chase monitors online sites for trucks. The commercial sites tend to focus on giant vehicles: 18-wheelers, big buses, even an occasional tank. (A used tank is an intriguing prospect for a design lab, but would send, perhaps, the wrong message rolling into a neglected neighborhood.) The most fruitful source of leads, for trucks of the size O+A is seeking, turns out to be the massive online flea market Craigslist. All kinds of ordinary folk, it seems, have old trucks to sell on Craigslist. Chase identifies at least a dozen for the 'truck review' meeting a week after kickoff. As the design team gathers in the conference room, he lays out photos on the big table.

A dozen existing conditions to choose from—take your pick!

Here's a 1990 ice cream truck for sale in Las Vegas for $9,800. Here's a 1965 stick-shift cutie in Salem, Oregon for $7,200. ("Who here can drive stick?" Verda asks. A few hands go up.) Here's a newer model, a 2002 USPS truck with a diesel engine available in Palm Springs for $8,000. As the options proliferate, what the truck will be, what the many members of the design team want it to be, becomes less and less

distinct. Interior design is a practical skill. Verda has noted on more than one occasion that designers are most comfortable solving problems. Give them a fait accompli to deal with—a specific set of dimensions, however problematic—and they will prove themselves endlessly inventive. But give them a blank slate—or too many choices—and... gulp!

The multiple set of existing conditions to choose from, combined with the number and variety of opinions, eventually stalls out the truck review meeting. Everyone is heard. Nothing is decided. Elizabeth volunteers to go to Palm Springs; Primo volunteers for Vegas. Everyone looks at everyone else, waiting for someone to strike a path forward. In the end it is agreed to continue the search, concentrating in the near term on options closer to home. A sensible move, but somehow after all the possibilities, anticlimactic. Even before the concept for the truck has fully flowered, practicality is rearing... well, no one wants to call it an 'ugly head.'

- - -

Gray skies and winter's first threat of rain hang over the Friday morning when Chase sets out to look at a step van for sale in South San Francisco. He has invited fellow designer George Craigmyle to make the trip with him. Together they form a team that would not be out of place in a BBC road series. Despite being born and raised in LA, Chase's family background is English and with his cloth cap, whiskers and easy manner he could pass for a London publican or cabbie. George really is from the UK, from Scotland, and his disarming Glaswegian brogue, paired with a lanky angularity, makes everything he says a lyric pleasure to American ears. Driving down from O+A's office in San Francisco to meet with Raymond Chuong, the seller of the truck, Chase and George talk fondly of old road trips in California and Scotland. One of the alluring elements of the Food for Thought Truck project is the idea of a design exercise turning into a road trip. This jaunt down the peninsula feels like a rehearsal for greater expeditions to follow.

After miles of talk and not-much-to-see, a street sign abruptly announces: "Downtown."

19

One of the alluring elements of the Food for Thought Truck project is the idea of a design exercise turning into a road trip. This jaunt down the peninsula feels like a rehearsal for greater expeditions to follow.

F
F
T
T

-

11
-
17

22

ꞃ ꞃ ꞃ "We're in Downtown now," George says. "Not sure Downtown of what city, but..."

The industrial districts to the south of San Francisco are as sprawling and formless as the city is compact. A flat landscape of warehouses and office parks, fast food eruptions and ceaseless freeway traffic, it could be the outskirts of any city in America—we might be in Phoenix, we might be in Cleveland. Such districts are the jetsam, economic and architectural, thrown off by deeply rooted urban centers. The randomness of the businesses here—an auto repair shop next to a trampoline manufacturer next to a granite and marble supply, all housed in featureless horizontal buildings—speaks to a human impulse that is the opposite of design. It is the primitive instinct to nest where you land, to occupy a space, any space, and make a go of it. Planners and architects decry the ugliness of these districts, their resistance to order, their apparent soullessness—but they are undeniably generators of prosperity. Step past any one of these nondescript facades and you will likely find a world you didn't know existed.

On their way to look at the truck, for example, Chase and George stop by a stone supply company to check out a slab of marble for another project. In the warehouse behind the showroom great planks of stone cut from quarries in northern Italy or the southern US are lined up like LPs in a giant used record shop. A potential buyer can flip through these LPs—but carefully; each one weighs about 900 pounds. Warehouse hands steer forklifts through the stacks picking out kitchen countertops and fancy reception facings for luxury projects. It's a bustling, thriving scene, not soulless at all, and it's a hint of what the Food for Thought Truck will be up against when it goes on the road. Designers love design, but the occupants of a space mostly care about its function.

In the parking lot outside the marble company Chase calls Raymond to say he and George are on the way. The agreed-upon meeting place isn't really a place—it's a stretch of pavement in back of a truck stop. Again, hard to visualize what 'design' could accomplish here. The utter lack of method in this landscape, and its aesthetic of pure expedience—highway, parking lot, train tracks, construction cranes—would appear to place it beyond salvation. But maybe that's what makes it the perfect birthplace for a mobile design lab, perfect in the sense that

movie monsters and superheroes often emerge from the ooze. Where better for a design crusade to begin than here at a kind of architectural Ground Zero?

The truck that finally pulls in from the street looks neither monstrous nor heroic. It's a plain white box on wheels with a wide, two-paned windshield and barn doors in the back that open outward—an advantage over the more common roll-up door, which, when open, consumes valuable interior space. The truck rolls to a stop and Raymond Chuong gets out. He too seems advantageously plain. Chase knows how he hopes to conduct himself during this meeting: "You really need to be critical when you're buying a vehicle. Keep your mouth shut. Think about everything you have to look at and make sure you capture everything." But when Raymond proves to be the same affable, hands-in-his-pockets, kick-the-gravel sort of guy as Chase and George, the negotiations take a decidedly informal turn.

"Wish I'd known what you guys had in mind," Raymond says after the project is explained. "I'd have cleaned it up for you." He seems at some pains to point out every flaw. "Don't mind the smiley faces," he

says of ink doodles on the interior walls of the truck. "That's just me being goofy." He has owned the truck for four years, has used it for his automotive service business. It shows the wear of steady use, but seems to be in pretty good shape. "All the lights work," he says, "I just don't know which switch does what."

George snaps photos while Chase does his due diligence. He looks under the hood. He checks the wheel wells. He gets into the back and examines every corner. He starts up the engine and listens to how it runs.

"George, race the motor for me."

Chase climbs down and George climbs up. He pumps the gas pedal to rev the motor while Chase holds his hand to the exhaust pipe, then brings his fingers to his nose.

"You're smelling for either a gasoline smell," he explains later, "or for an oil smell. If you're smelling gas, either the thing is running really rich, and there's a lot of gas being wasted or the timing is off or maybe the valves aren't adjusted correctly. Basically it's not running at peak performance. If you smell oil it means oil's leaking somewhere into the exhaust and that's

23

24

F
F
T
T

-

11

-

17

F
F
T
T
–
11
–
17

r r r a sign of something going bad. So what you want to smell is nothing. I mean you'll still smell something, but the lighter it is the better."

After his smell test, Chase and Raymond take the truck for a spin. On the open road it shakes and bucks like a stagecoach, but Chase cannot disguise his enjoyment in driving it. He gets it up to 40 mph. He honks the horn. ("Did that guy just flip us off?") By the time he pulls back into the truck stop where George is waiting—because not more than two people can ride in this truck at one time—heavy rain drops are pelting down. The first rain of the season! In drought-fearful California there could be no better omen. As the guys shake hands, noses dripping under the squall, it feels like a deal is near—or would be if the decision were being made today. Raymond has completely dropped his guard:

"Only thing that doesn't work is the radio," he says cheerfully.

———

Driving back to the office, Chase mulls over the practicalities of purchasing this truck: "If 10K is our budget and we get it for 8 or 7.5, we could put 3 or 4K into getting it tuned up. Maybe I'll dicker with Raymond a little."

"It would be rude not to haggle," George says.

"Whatever we put inside will have to be fastened down," Chase says. "It's pretty bouncy in there."

Is he rehearsing his haggle patter? It's clear he liked the truck, liked Raymond. But when he reports to Verda and Lisa, who will make the final call, he mustn't seem like a pushover.

"Do you feel like this is the one?" George asks.

"I'd like to say so."

"Shouldn't buy the first one you look at, but it did look good."

In the end it's the practicalities that give designers sleepless nights—the door that bumps the wall, the lighting fixture that generates glare on computer screens. Whatever imaginative transformation O+A's design team cooks up for the Food for Thought Truck, if the vehicle breaks down on the highway, everyone will turn to Chase. Like the 900-pound slab of marble he selected earlier in the day, his judgment now about the fitness of the truck will have real consequences for the project down the road. Literally down the road.

So is this the one?

"It smelled fine to me," he says.

"But maybe that's what makes it the perfect birthplace for a mobile design lab, perfect in the sense that movie monsters and superheroes often emerge from the ooze. Where better for a design crusade to begin than here at a kind of architectural Ground Zero?"

F F T T
T

11
–
17

27

Fortunately for the project Chase knows what he's looking at—and smelling.

The Concept

Brainstorming the pilgrimage.
Art or snark?
Kristina lists necessities.
A map makes it real.

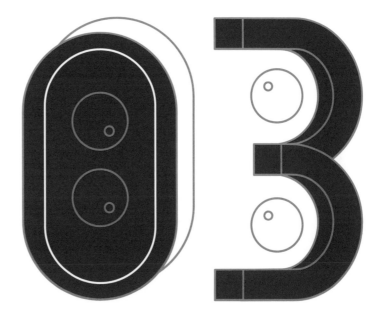

"How about this? We drive the truck to Silicon Valley and park it on one of the big tech campuses—Google or Apple or whatever—and we erect an O+A-designed office, but with one catch. All of the technology is analog. So it's typewriters, manual adding machines, rotary dial phones, tape recorders with audio tape, mimeograph machines, and we populate the office with elderly people and give them a specific task to do, perhaps produce a 'quarterly report,' which we sell to visitors and then we use the proceeds to give to the charity that buys computers for schools. We call it *Wave of the Future*."

Everyone laughs.

"The why needs to be really compelling," Primo had said at the kickoff, but over the next few weeks 'the why' of the Food for Thought Truck project proves elusive. While the broad idea of taking a design lab on the road to execute community-changing interventions sounds intriguing, as soon as you consider specific interventions in specific communities, things get more complicated. Will the truck be welcome? Will its work have meaning? What exactly can and should that work be?

Design is all about specifics. Indeed, the process of design could be described as the exercise of getting more and more specific within a broad physical framework—a floor, a suite, a room. It's no accident that the word designers use for choosing furniture or finishes is 'specify'—as in, "I'm specifying Herman Miller for the conference chairs." (Actually, "I'm 'spec'ing Herman Miller"—like other professions, design loves its jargon). This process of working toward greater definition and more precise detail is present both in the arc of every broad design project, and in a recurring pattern in each phase. During concept development O+A designers take a general understanding of the character and history of the client and refine it into a story that becomes the basis for the design. The Food for Thought Truck project is unique in that this story is not an abstraction but a series of actions yet to be performed. The concept requires not just metaphorical relevance, but practical

FFTT - 12 - 17

31

The challenge for
the team is to
choose projects
commensurate with
a small team's
ability to make
a difference.

feasibility, worthiness and impact. It's not just a concept —it's a plan of attack.

To help the team understand what is needed, Verda drafts a statement of purpose. As a fine artist who has shown in galleries and museums, she is not unfamiliar with the language of such statements:

The Food for Thought Truck will serve as a mobile office/design lab that will support a team of designers and artists who will infiltrate the community and enact projects of reclamation in the service of expanding our view of the world as we know it.

It's a canny declaration seeded with word choices designed to inspire. "Infiltrate" should appeal to those on the team who see this project as an adventure, a kind of design commando operation. "Enact projects of reclamation" speaks to the ecologists and urban planners in the group. And "expanding our view of the world as we know it" goes right to the sweet spot of the team's aspiring artists—which is to say, everybody. Still, as every team leader knows, inspiration is most effective as a motivator when accompanied by a kick in the seat of the pants. Perhaps that's why Verda attaches an assignment to her concept statement: "You guys should go out and look for things that need help." By which she means buildings or street corners or empty lots around the city (or any city) that the truck team might somehow interact with and transform. Everyone agrees to come back in a week with a specific mission for the truck.

For example... elderly people running mimeograph machines on the Google campus.

It is one week later. The team has gathered in the conference room, increasingly the 'war room' for the Food for Thought Truck project, to present ideas and pitch concepts. Some people have brought detailed visual presentations—image boards, sketches; others have jotted a few words on a card. *Wave of the Future* gets a laugh, but it's not really in the spirit imagined for the truck—too snarky, too smart-ass.

Closer to the mark is Marbel Calderon's idea of working with a homeless shelter. She has already reached out to Operation Dignity in Oakland, has already spoken to the Development Manager there, has already worked up a possible plan. "With our expertise and what we do daily," she tells the group now, "we can help them with lighting or effectiveness of space. And then I got to thinking that this could be a great opportunity to use the relationships that

we build with landlords and brokers because we specify all these fancy chairs and stuff and it gets trashed so quickly." Marbel's idea is to create a system of redistribution whereby furniture replaced in commercial design projects gets repurposed for use in homeless shelters.

It's a bold, ambitious, closely reasoned plan. And yet...

The reality of a design office is that the thing you have poured your heart into, the absolutely terrific idea you have worked out in detail, even to the extent of calling up the development manager—all of it can get blinked away with a casual, "It's a great idea, but..." The "but" here is homelessness. Is it the right issue for O+A? The homeless problem in San Francisco and Oakland is so deeply rooted, so tragic in its consequences, that one approaches it warily, aware of past failures. The Food for Thought Truck mustn't be seen as breezing into someone's personal life crisis with a week or two of 'design'. The problems the truck confronts need to be commensurate with O+A's ability to solve them. Homelessness feels too complex, too vast.

"Wow," Verda says after Marbel presents her concept. "I've been trying to stay away from political, but... I'm game." Tellingly, she adds, "If that's what we want to do."

– – –

As unfocused and inefficient and desultory as it may seem, the path to specificity in interior design is often conversation. Though Food for Thought Truck's weekly team meetings soon begin to feel repetitive—"We may not continue to meet weekly," Verda says—and the slow accumulation of ideas and winnowing of possibilities gradually gives the project a direction. Much of it comes from talking about specifics:

"Like for instance if we're going to be sleeping in [the truck] then that's going to be a large design feature," George Craigmyle says during a concept brainstorm early in December. Once again the team has assembled to toss around ideas for the project. The conundrum is that concept ideas can't take shape until the team knows what the truck is going to do—and the team can't know what it's going to do until there's a concept. To break the circle, the designers talk about what specifically will go into the truck, what furniture, what equipment. "If we're talking about printing or production or some form of fabrication," George continues, "again, that will be a large portion of the design."

"Do we need a workshop in there?" Rachelle Meneses says. Her job is to monitor time and budget on a project already two or three weeks behind schedule. "Are we just designing or are we also fabricating? I guess the question is what's our product? What's our deliverable?"

"I think we're delivering more than just drawings," Verda says. "More than just ideas. I think we want to make things. From what I'm hearing myself say—make things and leave things behind. Guerilla tactics. And maybe get arrested for them."

Lisa says, "Rachelle, add tickets and bail to the budget, please."

From what I'm hearing myself say—Verda's comment recalls Flannery O'Connor's line about why she writes: "I don't know what I think until I see what I say." This process of discovering by doing is how a lot of people write, paint, sculpt, compose music: a common creative process for solitary creators. But for collective forms of creativity, like interior design, the plunge-ahead-and-see-what-happens approach can be difficult to manage. For one thing, nine people in a room brainstorming for an hour represent nine hours of unbillable time. (Another reason Verda is thinking of killing the weekly meetings.) This is why designers love lists and spreadsheets, Google docs and Basecamp plans. The sooner order can be imposed on the process— or even the illusion of order—the better a team of problem solvers can feel about their progress.

"I made a list of necessities we know we're going to need," Kristina Cho says at the early December brainstorm. Kristina produces an artful food blog, Eat Cho Food, for which she collects the recipes, cooks the food, photographs the process and the result, and writes a witty commentary. No stranger, then, to organizing and executing complicated creative enterprises. "My list is: collaboration space, a work surface, tools, technology and then..." she lowers her voice, "...snacks." The team laughs. "Human comforts, you know? Insulation, good air, light. These are my necessities."

"And a fridge," George says.

Rachelle says, "Beer."

From these practicalities a mental image of the truck emerges. Whatever initial visions of a circus wagon or a traveling art gallery some on the team have entertained, a consensus is growing around an operation very similar to a food truck: a working 'kitchen' with all the appliances and implements necessary to cook up a design and serve it out the window. The idea sets some parameters around the concept, but until decisions are made and dimen-sions established, it will remain a mental image—actually nine mental images.

At a last Food for Thought Truck meeting before the Christmas break Verda brings in a rolled-up canvas and unfurls it on the conference table. A cry of delight goes up. It's a Rand McNally wall map of the United States. The last meeting ended in a funk—no truck purchased, no clear plan chosen for what the truck will do. Verda feared the team was becoming dispirited before the project could even get underway. This sudden unveiling of geographic possibility reignites the spark of inspiration. Where could we go? What could we do? The designers crowd around America.

"Where's Bakersfield?"

Kristina has identified a possible project in Bakersfield. Verda puts a tab on that Central Valley town.

"And we'll probably start our first project here." She puts a tab on the Bay Area.

"Where's Salt Lake?"

An O+A staffer currently working remotely from Utah is looking for a project there.

"And from there... Denver?"

"Where's Austin?" Verda says. "That might be our last stop."

"South by Southwest?"

"No, Primo's class."

Primo will teach a class in workplace design at the University of Texas, Austin this summer. While the class will end well before Food for Thought Truck can get to UT, there is some discussion of having the students launch a locally based project which the truck team can return to and bring to conclusion. It's a vague prospect at best, but Verda's tab in the center of the Lone Star State sends a buzz of excitement through the meeting. A long drive across the West Texas plains in August, conceivably in a vehicle without air conditioning, toward a goal not yet defined—at this point in the search for a concept (and a truck), that idea is just specific enough to get a room full of designers fired up.

F
F
T
T
-
12
-
17

33

The Sketches

How CAD killed the T-square.
Kristina's guide to freehand sketching.
The truck emerges in pen and pencil.

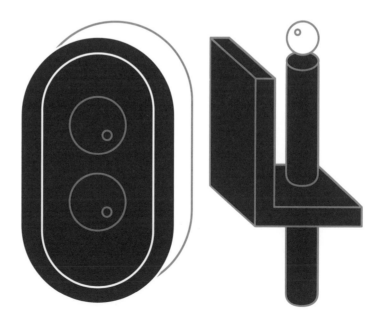

In 1963 a playful computer scientist from MIT named Ivan Sutherland presented his PhD thesis at the Spring Joint Computer Conference in Detroit, and quietly torpedoed a process of design that had been in place since the beginning of cities. The torpedo wouldn't hit for a few decades, but when it did, certain professions—architect, interior designer, graphic artist—would be changed forever.

Ivan Sutherland's thesis debuted his invention, Sketchpad, a program by which a person seated at a computer could apply a 'light pen' to a monitor and draw lines on the screen that the computer could then model into fixed geometries—exact angles, perfect circles. Once the computer had established a diagram, the light pen could then move it around, duplicate it, make it smaller or larger, or hook onto a corner of it and change its orientation or shape while every line adjusted accordingly. It was a startling demonstration of graphic elasticity, but the most remarkable thing about it was the way the person with the light pen and the computer interacted—which is to say directly, in the same way an artist interacted with... well, his sketchpad.

Despite its catchy name, Sketchpad never became a consumer electronics product, probably because in 1963 a computer powerful enough to perform its functions was the size of a utilities boiler in a multi-unit apartment building. Computers as consumer electronics were still about 15 years away. Still, if Ivan Sutherland's invention didn't immediately sweep the design world, hindsight detects in its debut the faintest first breath of an approaching hurricane. At the moment Sutherland was delivering his paper to fellow computer scientists in Detroit, an architect's office anywhere in the world was recognizably a configuration of drafting tables, large-format flat files, balsa wood models and drawing tools that had not significantly changed in centuries: pencils and erasers, crayons and chalk, measuring tape and masking tape, T-squares and compasses. And all of these things contributed to the mystique of the profession.

More than any other creative enterprise (with the possible exception of making movies) architecture,

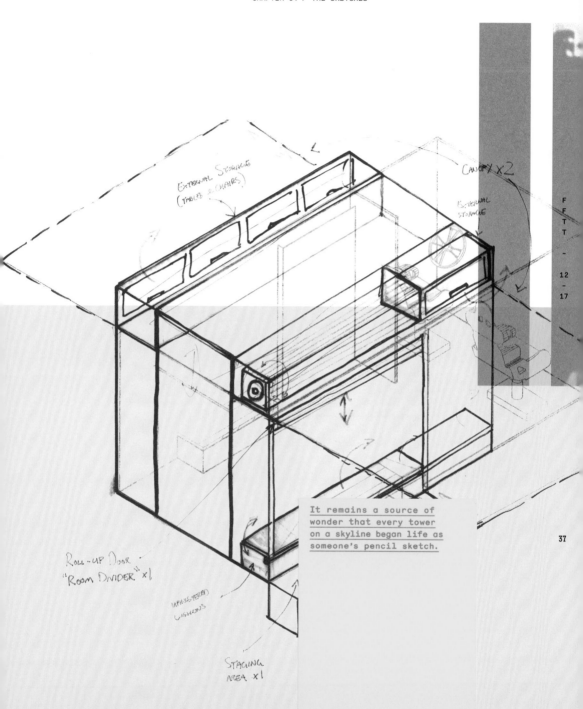

EXTERNAL STORAGE
(TABLES & CHAIRS)

CANOPY X2

EXTERNAL STORAGE

ROLL-UP DOOR
"ROOM DIVIDER" x1

UPHOLSTERED CUSHIONS

STAGING AREA x1

FFTT - 12 - 17

> It remains a source of
> wonder that every tower
> on a skyline began life as
> someone's pencil sketch.

37

F
F
T
T

-

12
-
17

Ivan Sutherland's
'Sketchpad' was
hardly a pad—but
it signaled the end
of drafting tables
and T-squares.

every time it was practiced, made a transit from art to science and back to art again, in a process that at its most sublime seemed like alchemy. Lines sketched freely on paper ignited a spark, the full blaze of which was then codified into calculations and measurements that, when handed to a builder, became… St Paul's Cathedral or Fallingwater or the Empire State Building. That the world's great cities were made of immense structures, each one of which began humbly in the movement of a pencil across a piece of paper, was one of civilization's enduring miracles. And it was precisely that marriage of art and science that made it so. No wonder the profession attracted people of wizardly temperament.

Ivan Sutherland's Sketchpad threatened to upend that magic. By placing science at the beginning of the process, automating (and eventually digitizing) the spark, computer-assisted design threatened to do to architecture what technology was, in fact, doing to the movies—take it away from the old-style wizards, swashbucklers, adventurers and crazy artists who had invented the industry and hand it over to the nerds. It didn't happen right away, and the actual system that emerged as the dominant designer's software grew from a different branch of computer science than the Sketchpad model, but Sutherland's breakthrough can be properly said to have revolutionized architecture and design. Drafting tables and T-squares were

doomed by Sutherland's PhD thesis. The word 'blueprint' dived toward obso-lescence. The process of how structures and their interiors were designed embarked on a course from which it could not turn back. Within 50 years of the Spring Joint Computer Conference in Detroit, design would be an entirely different profession.

Except for one thing.

- - -

It is mid-morning in December 2017. Kristina Cho sits at her workstation at O+A's office in San Francisco. As pioneers of open-plan design, O+A practices what it preaches. Two parallel sets of long shared tables run the length of the office from front staircase (the work studio is on the second floor) almost to the arched windows at the back. Designers are seated elbow-to-elbow on either side with only computer monitors to separate each person from the face of the person seated opposite. Even with the monitors between them awkward eye contact is a running joke at the company. Collaboration!

But Kristina is not in collaborative mode today. She has her headphones on. She's listening to a James Blake album in an effort to drown out the animated conversations around her. She has an image up on her computer of an ingeniously designed folding chair, but her keyboard is pushed aside. She is sketching.

On trace paper, with a pencil.

38

"I always like to sketch by hand at first," she explains later, "because I feel like if I start off on the computer I get really rigid and start modeling things in too much detail. It's not really the purpose of initial sketches to get too detailed." She is working on potential configurations for the Food for Thought Truck's interior—sketch after sketch of interlocking panels and tables that flip down from the wall. "I like a pencil—an actual pencil," she says of her drawing technique. "I do not like sketching with pen because I feel like it's a lot of commitment. I know some people like to use pen, because you get a kind of sketchy look—but I like just a soft pencil. And I use a lot of trace. I layer things. I like to mix and match and pull out a layer if I don't like it. Or put something else on top. I have this sheet of paper, with a rectangle on it and I just start layering trace, drawing over it, layering, layering, layering."

This exercise of trial and edit is, of course, the purpose of sketching and no doubt the reason why doing it by hand has held on through the computerization of every other step in the process. The quick rehearsal of an idea dashed in pencil on a sheet of paper; the swift subliminal decision-making entailed in chasing an accident of the pencil, trying a line that bends this way or that, arcs or doesn't arc, curves or shimmies free of logic or geometry. It affirms what even the nerdiest CAD-hand knows: that however powerful the computer's ability to process data, the human brain remains a far more subtle and surprising instrument of judgment. And given the proper talent and training, the alignment of that brain with a practiced hand can produce discoveries still beyond the reach of computer-assisted drafting. Collaboration!

"I'm drawing a box to scale at 12 by 6," Kristina says, "because I want to know this is what the size is going to be. Having a scale is really important so I can visualize how much room someone is going to have in a particular space. I draw things as close to scale as possible even if I'm just eyeballing it. And I sit there for a couple of hours and get everything out. Every idea that I have, I just sketch it out. If it's a table that folds I'm going to draw it just to see how it fits. And if it doesn't work I can throw it away, but at least I drew it."

Is she a confident artist? Does she draw well?

Kristina is from Ohio. She was raised to have modest Midwestern manners. But she is also a young woman in San Francisco where the culture is to assert your value. So her answer to the question is:

"Yes. (Pause). I guess so. (Pause). Yes."

She laughs.

"I do a lot of watercolor on the side," she continues. "Watercolor and pencil are probably my mediums of choice." Modestly, then, she makes it clear that she is absolutely comfortable in this milieu and that sitting down to sketch by hand with a soft pencil on sheets of trace paper is as natural to her as breathing. Then glancing around at all the noise and awkward eye contact in progress, she adds, "Ideally I would be by myself."

– – –

The early sketches that Kristina produces for the Food for Thought Truck focus on interior surfaces and installations that can morph from one form into another—a floor from which bench seating can be raised, a wall that can flop down on hinges and become an external platform for presentations, chairs and tables that fold into a flat butcher block. In the cramped confines of the truck's interior everything will have to multi-task. It's a necessity for the project, but it's also a tenet of O+A's aesthetic. In an era of accelerating change all spaces must be versatile. The truck thus becomes an abbreviated example of a larger design principle, precisely the sort of merging of thought and thing that O+A relishes.

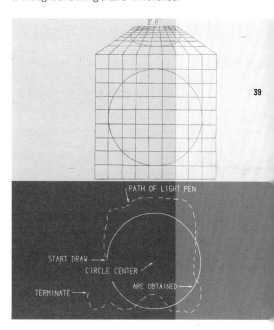

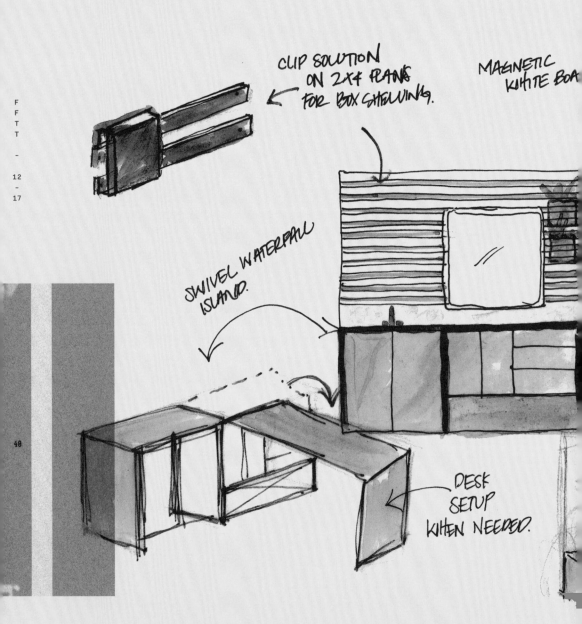

CLIP SOLUTION
ON 2X4 PLANKS
FOR BOX SHELVING.

MAGNETIC
WHITE BOA

F
F
T
T
-
12
-
17

SWIVEL WATERFALL
ISLAND.

40

DESK
SETUP
WHEN NEEDED.

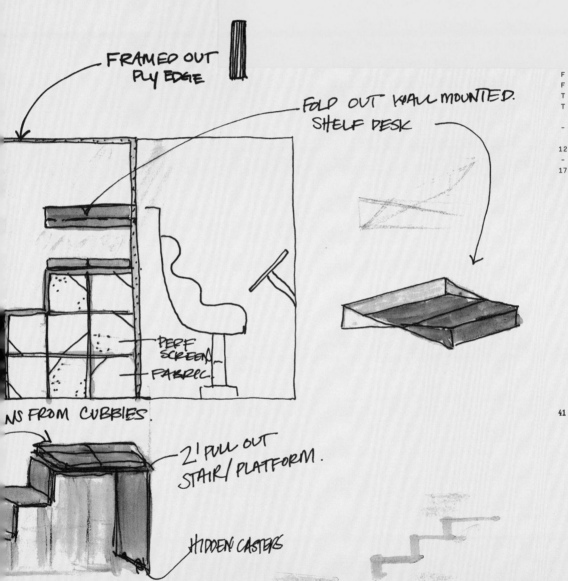

FRAMED OUT
PLY EDGE

FOLD OUT WALL MOUNTED.
SHELF DESK

FFTT
-
12
-
17

PERF
SCREEN
FABRIC

NS FROM CUBBIES.

21 PULL OUT
STAIR / PLATFORM.

HIDDEN CASTERS

41

"I always like to sketch by hand at first," she explains later, "because I feel like if I start off on the computer I get really rigid and start modeling things in too much detail. It's not really the purpose of initial sketches to get too detailed."

F
F
T
T
-
12
-
17

ᚱᚱᚱᚱ And Kristina's are not the only sketches in the works. George Craigmyle's concept drawings take the shape-shifting idea even further. His sketches of how a refitted truck might 'explode' outward, so that when parked and unpacked it surrenders its vehicular shape to become a kind of caravanserai encampment, carry the design beyond lines and planes to purpose.

You could call this George's forte as a designer. He began his career working for a fire-safety sprinkler company in Glasgow, Scotland. He trained in the literally life-and-death placement of complex sprinkler systems in the ceiling layouts of commercial and residential interiors, and can speak at length about how—despite what you've seen in the movie—a terrorist (or anti-hero) could not possibly set off a deluge by holding a cigarette lighter to a smoke detector. In short, George is a practical guy. Through the first weeks of the project his has been the voice calling everyone to earth when brainstorming sessions have spiraled into clouds of heroic conjecture over what the truck might do. His 'exploded truck' sketches may be the most radical yet in design terms, but they also envision the practical dimension of how the design will be put to use: an encampment to unfold here, people to gather there...

That same pragmatism informs the sketches George does with fellow designer Nikki Hall to determine how the truck will fit on O+A's small parking lot. In a city where parking is practically a cryptocurrency, O+A's South of Market (SOMA) office with its own tiny parking lot in the front is a major perk for the company's principals and a convenience for visiting clients and product reps. It has also

42

become a gathering place for staff on sunny days. There's a picnic table and a barbecue grill. There are planter boxes and a bicycle rack. The introduction of a food truck parked for months in this space threatens to disrupt the spatial economy. In the earliest weeks of the project, George and Nikki go out and take laser measurements of the lot, with the sole purpose of devising a scheme by which Primo and Lisa will still have room to park their cars and co-principal Perry Stephney will have space for his motorcycle. (As champion of the truck and the only principal regularly willing to take BART, Verda is not so concerned with parking.) Once an accurate schematic of the lot is in hand, George and Nikki sketch in the truck at various orientations to determine how best to preserve Big Cheese dominion.

Or rather they sketch an estimation of the truck. All across the project Kristina's sketches, George's sketches, Nikki's and Marbel's and Verda's sketches remain, for the moment, purely speculative—because O+A does not yet have a truck. Despite passing the smell test, Raymond Chuong's step van slipped away a couple of weeks after Chase and George made the trip to South San Francisco to check it out. Raymond sold to another buyer before Verda and Lisa could close the deal. The original project schedule called for the truck to be purchased and in hand by the end of November. Now with Christmas approaching, Chase is again canvassing the Internet. Rachelle is eyeing the schedule nervously. And the rest of the design team continues to spin in perpetual sketch phase. Sketching is pleasure, but everyone is eager, even the watercolorists are eager, to move from the art to the science of design. That can't happen until there are actual dimensions to work with, actual volumes to be filled, actual angles and planes. It can't happen until O+A buys a truck.

F
F
T
T

-

12
-
17

44

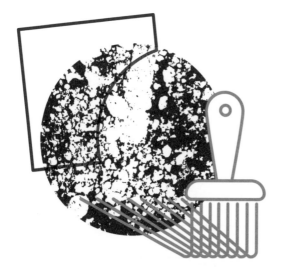

F
F
T
T

-

12

-

17

FOOD FOR THOUGHT TRUCK MISSION :   EMPOWER PEOPLE TO BE CREATORS , DESIGNERS

THE IDEA COLLECTOR

COLLECT IDEAS FROM ONE SITE , BRING THEM TO THE NEXT

DRAW PEOPLE IN BY PROVIDING A COOL , COMFORTABLE PLACE TO EAT
FOOD TRUCK FOOD

INTERACTIVE EXCHANGE OF IDEAS : DRAWING , BUILDING , VIRTUALLY DE

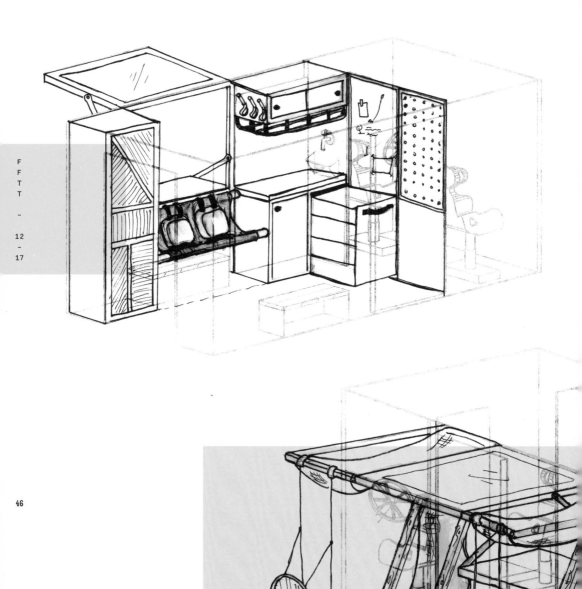

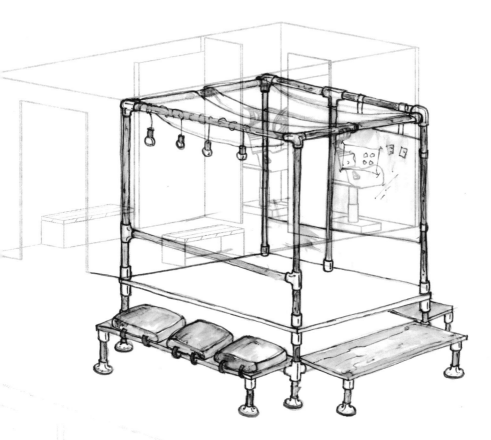

F
F
T
T
-
12
-
17

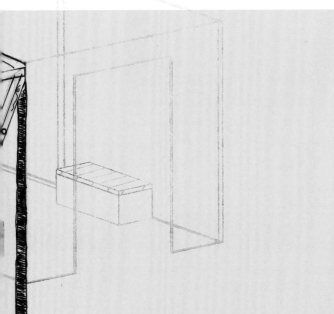

In sketch after
sketch designers
rehearse the
ways the truck
might unfold.

The Truck II

Mid-life course correction as a force for good.
Chase and Verda test an ice cream truck.
A Christmas delivery comes late.

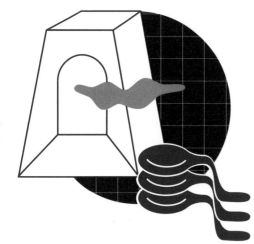

F
F
T
T
-
12
-
17

A bright, brisk morning in the East Bay. There has not been nearly enough rain this winter, but on a day like today the promise of California shines with ever-renewable optimism. Here is an element of invention seldom given its due—the impact of place. In the Bay Area openness to new thinking and new ways of doing things has been a point of regional identity since the Gold Rush days. It has shaped the area's cultural, sexual and political character. It has surely been a factor in the explosion of entrepreneurship that now gives this part of California the hottest economy in the nation. While it's true that the explosion created its own intractable problems—an affordable housing crisis, an epidemic of homelessness, growing class resentments—the subliminal knowledge that your bright idea can actually take root here is a powerful counterweight to whatever obstacles the local real-estate market presents to daily living. Combine that with the region's natural assets—the Bay, the sky, the light, the fresh air—and you have a remarkably congenial environment for getting up each morning to try something new.

Chase and Verda are traveling to Berkeley today to look at a step van that has just cropped up on Craigslist. Pulling onto a cozy, tree-lined street, they spot the truck parked in a driveway and the seller standing outside waiting. He waves as they drive by.

"Probably not a great idea to come over in a Porsche," Verda says. She has driven her personal vehicle to the meeting, forgetting that she will likely want to dicker about the price.

Alex Nerguizian waits by the truck as Verda and Chase walk back from their parking spot. Alex is a financial consultant in the throes of a mid-life... well, he prefers to call it an 'adventure.' After years of working in finance, he has decided to make a career U-turn and launch a gelato and espresso truck. He purchased the vehicle a month ago, then found out it did not meet code. By California law a truck serving food must have a minimum ceiling height of 74 inches. Alex's truck inside is 73 inches.

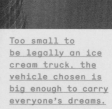

F
F
T
T

12
-
17

51

Too small to
be legally an ice
cream truck, the
vehicle chosen is
big enough to carry
everyone's dreams.

52

F
F
T
T
-
12
-
17

ᚱ ᚱ ᚱ His options are:

    A. Sell the truck and buy another

    B. Pay to have the ceiling raised

    C. Forget gelato and stick with finance

"Good morning!"

    Handshakes and introductions. Alex opens up the back of the truck and Verda and Chase climb inside. This truck is newer and cleaner than Raymond Chuong's stagecoach was—and looks to be in better condition, though a bit smaller, perhaps (that 73-inch ceiling could be a scalp scraper for someone, say, of George Craigmyle's height). Still, it's recognizably a superior vehicle. And as Verda and Alex chat...

    "What are you going to do with the truck?" he asks.

...it becomes clear this mid-life adventure works both ways. For a while now Verda has wanted to break free from the constraints of commercial design. The been-there-done-that factor has grown stronger with every corporate makeover or venture-funded start-up. Lately she has begun to question the very foundations of O+A's aesthetic: the comfort-zone workplace, the environment that offers so many distractions, so many seductions, from cafés to nap rooms that users are encouraged to stick around the office 24/7. "Who really works for 24 hours?" she told *Metropolis Magazine* in a recent interview. "What we should be designing are spaces to get your work done and go home."

    A couple of years ago Verda took a sabbatical from the company to work on sculpture and mixed media pieces at home in Orinda. She soon found she did not like the isolation of being an artist alone in her studio. Coming back during a season of crisis when a portion of the staff broke off to start their own (competing) company, she was driven for some months by the necessity of keeping the ship upright, but now that O+A is again on course, winning big contracts and winning awards, the old restlessness has returned. The lure of the Food for Thought Truck for Verda is precisely what it is for Alex Nerguizian—not gelato, not espresso, but freedom.

    After a short test drive Chase delivers his verdict: "It's pretty dang quiet." He does not bother with the smell test.

    This truck is about five thousand dollars more expensive than the first one, which means three thousand dollars over budget. Back at the office, Verda and Lisa huddle over the numbers, determined to act quickly this time, determined not to let the project fall further behind. Chase calls Alex that day with an offer and they agree to meet again the following day to finalize the paperwork. Everything is on track—until suddenly it isn't. Getting the check cut, the vehicle inspected and the insurance activated takes more than one day, and that is just long enough for a snag to develop.

    On the Friday before Christmas Lisa comes into the office from what should be her day off to deal with the crisis. Despite being the new steward of O+A's financial health and a designer and businesswoman with years of experience running huge projects, Lisa's manner is as easy and down-to-earth as your rambunctious big sister's. She is dressed in a sweatshirt, jeans and sneakers with a red sock cap pulled over her ears. After a brief discussion with Chase and O+A's Controller Mike Griffin on where the banking stands, Lisa places a call to Alex Nerguizian. Sitting on the floor with her phone, she might be talking to a little brother in trouble with Mom and Dad. "I understand completely," she says. A few of the team have gathered around. "Absolutely. Makes good sense." She listens for a moment and then says, "Okay, well you have a happy holiday and we'll talk again next week." She remains on the floor, forearms folded across her knees, looking up at the team. "He wants to think it over. He's getting cold feet. He thinks he might want to keep the truck." A collective groan moves through the office. "He said if he sells it to anyone he'll sell it to us, but he wants to think about it over the weekend. He's fallen in love with his truck." She shrugs. "I wouldn't worry. There was a kid crying in the background all through the conversation. He'll think about it over the weekend. He'll get his Christmas bills. He'll come around."

- - -

On 29 December 2017, O+A's Food for Thought Truck rolls onto the Tehama Street lot to a smattering of applause. It's just a smattering because most of the staff are away for the holidays and only a few people are on hand to come down and see for themselves the company's latest experimental project. Chase at the wheel honks the horn as he eases the truck across several parking spaces—again, thanks to the season there are no other cars on the lot today. Marbel riding in the passenger's seat takes video of the reception. After their applause the little audience lines up to 'tour' the truck, a process that entails, climbing into

F
F
T
T

-

12
-
17

54

O+A owns a truck. Having that option closed will presumably put an end to the second guessing, personal doubts and indecision that have plagued the early weeks of design development.

the back, testing the top of your head to make sure it's not in contact with the ceiling (73 is not a lot of inches) walking three or four steps forward to the driver's seat, turning around, walking three or four steps back, climbing out of the truck.

For the designers on staff who have not been part of this project and have heard it referred to only in passing, seeing the actual truck does not do much to clarify what exactly is going on here. This small step van, perfect for selling gelato (okay, an inch shy of perfect), does not immediately present itself as a mobile design lab. Is it big enough? Can its box shape be altered sufficiently to make it interesting? Would you want to ride for very long distances in this vehicle?

And yet, for the people on the Food for Thought Truck team, the arrival of the truck marks a significant milestone. On the one hand it is the point of no return. If at any time during these first weeks, Verda or Lisa entertained pulling the plug on the project, that option is now closed. O+A owns a truck. Having that option closed will presumably put an end to the second guessing, personal doubts and indecision that have plagued the early weeks of design development. More positively, having the truck in hand means the design challenge is finally defined. Now the designers, in Verda's formulation, will have specific problems to solve. Yes, the truck is a little smaller than some on the team envisioned, but the compactness of the space establishes at the outset that this will be an exercise in structural multi-purpose, that it's going to require economy and creative vision within tight parameters. What's that quote attributed to Orson Welles? "The enemy of art is the absence of limitations."

Nor are the food truck's limitations restricted to size. The internal layout of the truck imposes a few

existing conditions that will have to be incorporated into the design. For example, on either side of the interior, two rectangular boxes rest on the floor. These boxes cannot be moved. They are wheel wells, the casings inside of which the tops of the back tires move. Similarly the low ceiling is welded to the frame of the truck in a way that will make raising it a major structural rebuild—probably prohibitively expensive. Some early sketches imagined sliding the floor out to make an external platform or popping off the ceiling to let the sun shine in; some opened up the truck like a flower bursting from a bulb; some damn near had the thing taking wing. To see the real truck squatting in O+A's parking lot with its husky box frame, immovable wheel wells and low brow ceiling is to get back to the reality of space design.

Perhaps that reality is the most significant milestone achieved today. As Orson Welles knew, every creative enterprise begins in the mind twice the size and many watts brighter than what the final product will turn out to be. The moment at which a filmmaker begins to shoot footage, or a writer begins to cover a blank page with text or a designer begins to make drawings within assigned parameters, is the true beginning of creation. Most artists feel relief at this point. Most are happiest in the grease and dust of actual production. Chase's toot of the horn, while pulling onto O+A's parking lot, signaled his arrival and the true beginning of the project. It was also very probably a honk of relief.

F
F
T
T

–

12

–

17

55

The Visit

Maybe you CAN go home again.
An architect presents his project.
The truck scores a destination: Bakersfield!

You Can't Go Home Again is the title of a book by a now largely forgotten author, Thomas Wolfe, who wrote logorrheic novels in the 1920s and 30s and added years to his literary reputation by dying of tuberculosis at age 37. Wolfe's book may not be much read anymore, but his title has become an accepted nugget of popular wisdom: if you leave the place that made you, the wider world will seduce you away from its charms and you will never be able happily to return. In a city like San Francisco or LA or New York so many people are living that narrative that few have the perspective to question its premise.

Daniel Cater is one who did.

In 2015, after several years practicing architecture in Copenhagen and San Francisco, Daniel returned to his home town of Bakersfield, California, specifically for the purpose of bringing his expertise back to the place where it first showed promise. "It's kind of expected that if you go to college and you study something like architecture you're not coming back," he says of his hometown. "I watched the people that I went to high school with, and they're making Boston a better place, they're making Manhattan better, they're making San Francisco better. Meanwhile the place that meant so much to us and formed so much of who we are isn't really benefiting from that initial investment of the first 18 years of our lives."

Bakersfield is a city in the San Joaquin Valley a couple of hours north of Los Angeles, a Gold Rush town that turned into a commercial crossroads and became a hub for agriculture and energy production. It is one of those horizontal cities common in the American West that assemble under a capacious sky a collection of cultural elements so random that their convergence in one place defies logic: one of the world's largest producers of carrots; one of the country's largest producers of oil; home to proud Basque, Greek and Iranian communities; an enthusiastic auto racing town, a boxing town, a country music town.

In the 1950s a major earthquake and its aftershocks destroyed much of Bakersfield's historic architecture. Vacant lots created by that disaster remain to this day.

01
–
18

61

Thomas Wolfe's
'You Can't Go Home
Again' was once
a popular book,
but its titular
thesis may no
longer apply.

F
F
T
T

–

01

–

18

The city grew from a population of 57,000 in 1960 to 376,000 by 2016, so it is hardly moribund, but the skeins of creativity moving through its cultural life—theater and visual arts, homegrown retail, homegrown cuisine—never came together in a coherent civic identity. It is the sort of town that, if you're passing through, you might think, *Nothing here*—unless you stop for a sundae at the soda fountain in Dewar's Candy Shop, or for a beer at Guthrie's Alley Cat on Wall Street, and sense a more deeply rooted culture than meets the eye.

Daniel Cater's idea of going home to Bakersfield to help that culture assert itself falls into a broad category of rebirth and renewal that may or may not be the next trend in American urban development, but has produced hopeful results in recent years. The highest-profile examples are regional renaissances in mid-sized cities—Pittsburgh's rebound from the death of the steel industry, the blossoming of old cities across the South, the efforts to save Detroit.

When Daniel returned to Bakersfield from San Francisco some of his old mentors were surprised to see him back home. But, reaching out to like-minded creatives, he discovered in the local professional communities a common appetite for turning the page to Bakersfield's next chapter. As part of that effort, Daniel's company Cater Design Group produced the 17th Place Townhomes. Built mysteriously not on 17th but on 18th Street, the townhomes were not radical designs by San Francisco or Copenhagen standards, but in their embrace of smaller living,

green living, modern lines and a distinctly urban orientation they represented a new direction for Bakersfield. Daniel admits to wondering initially what the market would be. He was surprised by how quickly 17th Place filled up. "We kind of thought it would just be millennial transplants, but there are twelve children that live in the project, there are empty-nesters and retirees—you know, people that have the choice and demographics to be in large gated communities and instead they choose to live downtown."

Across a parking lot from 17th Place Daniel developed another you-CAN-go-home-again project with a young married couple coming back to California after several years of working in the restaurant business in Manhattan. There are 21 Starbucks in Bakersfield, but Café Smitten was the first neighborhood hangout of its kind, the sort of quirky coffee shop where regulars assume subliminal ownership and internalize the café's rhythms into their own. In that respect it was a prototype for what Daniel and his colleagues hoped to do on a grander scale with their Sleeping Beauty town.

"What I love about Bakersfield," Daniel says, "is there's this beautiful community, this beautiful spirit, but it's not conveyed yet in a way that gives it credit; it's not conveyed in a way that is easily understood." That then is the lure—along with the tug of family and affordability and all the rest, there is plenty in Bakersfield for an ambitious young architect to do.

– – –

"One thing that's nice is that the sidewalks are 14 feet wide."

Daniel and the Food for Thought Truck team are studying photographs of the parking lot between the townhomes project and Café Smitten on 18th Street. At Kristina's invitation (they used to work together at BAR Architects), he drove 300 miles north to San Francisco this morning to show the team these pictures and pitch this lot as an ideal site for the truck's first project in the field.

"You can see it's not in the best shape," he says of the lot. "The concrete's kind of cracked and old."

"It sounds like it's highly utilized," Verda says.

"It is highly utilized."

"So if we took over all of it we'd have angry people?"

Daniel tips his head to one side as if to suggest maybe not. It is clear from his imperturbable manner that turning angry people into allies is a skill he has developed along with architecture. "What if it was something long and linear?" he says. His idea is to

"There are 21 Starbucks in Bakersfield, but Café Smitten was the first neighborhood hangout of its kind, the sort of quirky coffee shop where regulars assume subliminal ownership and internalize the café's rhythms into their own."

F
F
T
T

-

01

-

18

keep the parking lot functioning, but make the space along the sidewalk some kind of living expression of Bakersfield's potential. He calls it "creating life between moments." A street festival, a greenspace, a row of benches—the precise nature of the intervention will emerge as Food for Thought Truck and Bakersfield launch their collaboration. But if for one week this summer the 17th Place Townhomes and Café Smitten are connected by a bridge of possibilities, this block of downtown may serve as inspiration to all the folks in Bakersfield with big plans for the city's revitalization.

It is just what the Food for Thought Truck team has been looking for. From the first kick-off meeting, where the truck would go and what it would do has been unclear. Today it comes into sharp, bright focus: a cracked parking lot on a sunbaked street in Bakersfield. You would think the team had landed a contract in midtown Manhattan. Around the conference table palpable excitement grows. Daniel has succeeded in selling the designers not only on his project, but on their own. The specificity of his pitch—this city, this parking lot—at last steers the truck onto a discernable path, gives it a purpose that is more than a 'concept.' Purchasing the Chevy made the Food for Thought Truck real as a design problem. Daniel's visit makes it real as a crusade.

And like all crusades 'the Bakersfield project,' as it comes to be known from this day forward, promises to be equal parts slog and poetry. For some at the table the slog is itself an attraction. It is a

designer's inclination to fall in love with unpromising spaces, to see in them not what everyone else sees, but what they might be. The grind of making that transformation happen is for such a person an invigorating workout of the sort that makes you stronger, makes you better at what you do. The poetry of the project emerges both from Daniel's personality —a native affability sharpened by those years in Europe and the Bay Area—and the guileless romanticism of his mission. "I always tell people if I never left Bakersfield I would never be able to do what I'm doing," he says. "I wouldn't know how to. I do think there is something about a process of going away and coming back." And his point is so provocative, his confidence so infectious that all around the table O+A staffers are thinking: Could I go home to Ohio? Could I go home to Missouri?

"This is why we want to pop off the roof," Kristina says, standing next to Daniel.

The meeting adjourned, a few members of the team have stepped out to take a look at the vehicle. Daniel is standing inside the truck with his head again tipped to one side, this time to avoid not angry people, but the aluminum ceiling. He is six feet, four inches tall.

"Really? Is that easy to do?"

"It's doable. Whether it's easy or not that's another question."

Outside the sirens of downtown San Francisco contribute their daily soundtrack of crisis. Along Tehama Street the midday addicts are passed out on sidewalks nowhere near 14 feet wide. Even beautiful cities wrestle with afflictions—but, yes, of course, everything is doable. If you have the time and the money and most of all the determination, there are no limits, history tells us, to how radically you can change your environment. It's just a matter of how tenacious you are at clinging to a vision and how much discomfort, ridicule, frustration you can swallow while it goes through cycles of progress and setback. Daniel looks none too comfortable right now, but he is smiling and moving around the truck's interior, scoping out its possibilities, calculating how they might fit into his plans—while trying not to bang his head against the ceiling.

"This is making me envious of short people," he says.

F
F
T
T
-
01
-
18

Daniel Cater envisions
Food for Thought Truck
parking near Café
Smitten, a popular
Bakersfield hangout
at the heart of an
emerging neighborhood.

The Program

George and Nikki pitch less-is-more.
Furniture takes shape as partnerships wobble.
Verda recalls a river journey.

F
F
T
T

–

01
–
18

70

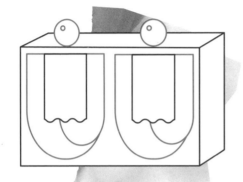

"We need to pop up the roof—for sure," Kristina says.

It is a few days after Daniel Cater's visit and the design team has come together again to look at progress, talk about direction and identify any issues that may have surfaced. It's a bright, brisk morning so the meeting takes place outside at the picnic table.

"Right now it's about 6 feet," Kristina continues.

George levels his palm over his head. "I think I've got an inch to spare."

"I feel like we need to pop it up at least another 18 inches. Just to be comfortable."

The vocabulary of design is relentlessly breezy. What does it take? Pop out some windows? Rip out a wall? Reducing complex construction operations into simple action verbs—pop, rip, throw—is the industry's professional shorthand. For an interior designer the world as it exists is always revisable. "Do I need to throw another hundred grand at it?" a property developer once said to Primo vis-à-vis a space he didn't like.

Today's conversation is rattling along heedlessly in this way when Verda makes a tea-kettle-coming-to-a-boil sound. "I do think we need to be conscious of *cost*," she says, the word 'cost' being the point at which the kettle whistles. It is Verda's onerous duty always to hold back heedless brainstorming with the tight reins of financial reality. "That's why the guy got rid of this truck, right? Because the ceiling was too low?"

"It was off by one inch."

"And the cost of raising it was more than he wanted to pay," Verda says. Her point is clear—if it was more than he wanted to pay, it's more than we want to pay. Not a project, then, you can throw a hundred grand at.

"Or maybe just the centerpiece," Kristina presses. "Kind of a pop-up in the middle so at least you have some comfortable headspace." It's not apparent how that modification—tall people in the center, short people on the perimeter—will be any less expensive than raising the roof from corner to corner, but the

FFTT
-
01
18

71

From figuring how much they can fit into the truck, the design team moves to how much they can leave out.

F
F
T
T
-
01
-
18

DESIGN SWA

Nikki and George
are tasked with the
important job
of finding room
for the truck
without sacrificing
parking for O+A's
principals.

thought allows the team to continue cutting metal in their daydreams a bit longer.

"We could do the moon if we had tons of money," Verda says.

– – –

In the early weeks of 2018 all the daydreaming about how to alter the truck, what it will look like, where it will go, returns from the moon and begins to get grounded in the hard dirt of existing conditions: cost, time, feasibility. Late in January O+A Design Director Mindi Weichman calls a pin-up meeting with Food for Thought Truck's designers in order to, as she puts it, "come back to Verda next week and show her we can make progress." Technically, Mindi is not part of the Food for Thought Truck team, but having guided the firm successfully through complex projects for Nike in Portland and New York, she has earned a reputation for stellar project management, and for that reason Verda has tapped her to get the truck out of 'park.'

The team gathers in O+A's big kitchen to pin up sketches of what they've been working on. While they pin, Mindi explains the agenda. "I want to get your take on what you think are reasonable deliverables. I think we can write a little to-do list for ourselves so it's clear we have it together and have a plan for how to accomplish things. Whoever wants to start—jump in."

George and Nikki go first. They have been a team since they partnered last month to take measurements of the parking lot in advance of the truck's arrival. They've been working on the interior floor plan ever since, and the sketches they're presenting today are notably simpler than some earlier, more densely furnished versions. "As far as space planning the truck previously," George says, "I think we've kind of chucked that out the window." He turns to the austere sketch on the wall. "I think the new direction we want to go is the truck is completely empty."

"It just hauls things around?" Mindi says.

"Exactly."

In those earlier iterations George and Nikki made space for two passenger seats in the back, along with cabinetry, a workshop with maybe a tool wall and a printer of some kind, perhaps even a 3D printer; also a counter that could double as an eating area and a mini-kitchen with small fridge and sink. Presumably it was getting a bit tight back there, but more alarming than the spatial economy was the conceptual economy. Were these designs in line with the purpose of the truck? Did they really represent what Food for Thought Truck wanted to be?

"We talked about the idea of the nomad," Nikki says, "and the bare human essentials that you might need. We talked about if you're a nomad and all you have is this truck and you're driving around what's

72

the first thing you do when you stop? You make shelter is the first thing. And the next thing is you eat food. And the next most important thing is to be in a community of people."

"And the thing we kept coming back to," George says, "was the camper van."

It was not where they wanted conceptually to land. After all the high level thinking, all the aspirational brainstorming about social outreach and urban planning, and making communities better through design, a Winnebago parked in an overcrowded campground was nobody's idea of Food for Thought Truck's destination. Drawing on desert Bedouins, then, and the plains Indians and herdsmen on the Mongolian steppes, George and Nikki pulled the truck free from its 'camper van' inclinations, to a purer, more aesthetically sustainable vision of nomadism. One thing all those transient cultures had in common during their nomadic heydays was a profoundly minimal regard for physical possessions.

"So basically what we're providing for you guys is an empty truck," Nikki says.

George says, "You're welcome."

– – –

In the pause after the laughter subsides Marbel asks, "So it no longer has cabinets?"

Nikki says, "Nope."

Marbel and Kristina have just spent the week designing mobile furniture and accessories that will require some kind of storage. A truck without cabinets is not going to cut it. Mindi weighs in: "I agree we don't want it to turn into a camper, but I do think we should maybe consider a wall of storage. If you think about driving this thing around—it's bumpy and who knows what's going to happen on the inside? You are going to want stuff that closes down and doors that lock or latch." Essential to the designer's craft is this ability to leap off the page of an elegant idea to its possibly less elegant practical application, and anticipate the obstacles that will be thrown in its way and the things that are going to break and not work.

"I like it being open and bare," Kristina says, "but I think getting completely rid of everything…"

She doesn't have to finish the sentence. George and Nikki quickly clarify that it was not their intention to have nothing at all in the truck, only that it be stripped down in the way a Shakespearean stage is stripped down so it may be adapted to multiple uses—Caesar's

Rome one night, Birnam Wood the next. With that stipulation agreed to by all parties, Marbel and Kristina proceed with presenting their designs to the team. Marbel has been working on the storage problem, a wall structure for hanging foldable furniture, a tile mat for stacking cushions that could be used in lieu of seating—very much in line with George and Nikki's nomad concept. Kristina shows her designs for modular furniture that can be assembled in different configurations. If the truck is going to spill out at each stop and become a little plaza of activity, the shape needs to be changeable. Kristina has come up with a triangular design that can be assembled to form rectangles and squares or long, snake-like, vertebrae seating.

Mindi says, "I feel like you guys should build one out of foam or chipboard or something. I think if you could come into our meeting next Tuesday with these ideas, but just build them—and it might be that by building them we find out that some of them are too complicated. But I think having some physical stuff to play with will go a long way."

"I can easily make a little half-scale truck," George volunteers. He is always happy in three dimensions.

"And it can be super simple, George," Mindi says. "I think it would help everybody get their heads around what parts of the truck are open and what parts fold out and stuff like that."

Kristina tries to remember. "Did we get a no about raising the roof?"

"We didn't get a hard no," George says.

Someone says, "Did we get a hard yes?"

– – –

If the design of the truck and its furnishings are finally acquiring clear lines and solid shapes, where it will go continues to be amorphous. Almost from the start the operational programming has followed a pattern of scaling back. That day when Verda unrolled a map of the US on a conference room table was the day of Food for Thought Truck's widest geographical scope. Texas was in the running that day. Nebraska was in the running. There was talk of Chicago. But as soon as the team applied the same critical analysis to the itinerary that Mindi used on the space plans and furniture specifications, the mileage on the truck's hypothetical odometer spun backward.

"If you think about driving this thing around," Mindi had said, and it is that thinking that eliminates the far-afield destinations. Drive this thing 1,700

Kristina and George
consistently balance
radical design with
practical ends—a
truck that not only
wows, but works.

75

ʳ ʳ ʳ miles from San Francisco to Austin in summer heat with no air conditioning? Drive it 2,100 miles across the Sierras, the Rockies and the western prairie to Chicago with—what?—two or three passengers illegally bouncing around in the back? Do you then drive it another 2,100 miles home? Does it break down on some windy stretch of Wyoming interstate far from any town, let alone any airport?

It is these considerations that lead the program planners quickly to limit Food for Thought Truck's reach to California—these and the obvious judgment that securing viable local partners is going to be easier in San Francisco or across the Bay in Oakland. Or so one would think. In the weeks that the design team is wrestling with the physical structure of the truck, the programming team wrestles with the Bay Area's recalcitrant nonprofit scene. What Food for Thought Truck's would-be do-gooders discover is that doing good in the Bay Area takes connections. Say you want to design a mini-park in a rough alley in San Francisco's Tenderloin. There are city-sanctioned organizations that facilitate such things, but they have a proposal process and a submission schedule that Food for Thought Truck has already missed for the year. Say you want to help a SOMA arts nonprofit give their annual block party a more attractive infrastructure? They are happy to accept the help, but there may not be a block party this year—they will have to get back to you. Verda connects with some nonprofits in Oakland that look promising—an art gallery, a children's book publisher. She gets a mildly receptive response, but there's an arm's length quality to their interest that stalls the collaborations before they get started.

The keenest enthusiasm, oddly, comes from the south. Nikki and O+A staff writer Al McKee have been looking into possible projects in Los Angeles. Geographically it makes sense that Food for Thought Truck's first season begins in San Francisco and ends in LA. There's a nice cultural symmetry to bookending the truck's California adventure between the State's two premier cities. And Los Angeles, surprisingly, turns out to be the more hospitable of the two.

Nikki has reached out to Helen Leung at LA Mas, a nonprofit dedicated to helping "lower income and underserved communities shape their future through policy and architecture." Helen was receptive, but as she and Nikki sorted out timeframes and the specific needs of each organization, it became clear LA Mas had nothing on the horizon that was going to work. Even so Helen sent Nikki a list of Los Angeles nonprofits that might partner with Food for Thought Truck and offered to introduce her to any that looked interesting.

At the programming meeting today Nikki and Al present the two most promising candidates. The Los Angeles Food Policy Council's projects seem a likely fit—programs to help corner grocers feature healthier food, an advocacy campaign to change city ordinances against food carts. It all chimes nicely with a converted food truck's new social activist life. And the other organization, River LA, appeals to the truck's identity as a truck. The Los Angeles River runs 51 miles through the heart of the city. River LA's mission is to create a coalition of the communities it touches to promote restoration of the river. It has worked with Frank Gehry to draw up a master plan, but there is much to be done in community outreach, and a truck that can drive the full 51 miles could be a valuable tool in that effort.

"I have a fun story about the LA River," Verda says. "When I left Harvard, SCI-Arc [the Southern California Institute of Architecture] was putting on this amazing thing—I'm so glad I did it—ten weeks with ten LA architects. And it was like Neil Denari and Antoine Predock and Michael Rotondi. NOT Frank Gehry, Frank Gehry did not participate, but—it was really incredible—Lebbeus Woods." As she speaks the whole universe of LA shapeshifters, the architects who put the ever-morphing landscape of Los Angeles into bending, slipping, avalanching buildings, springs to mind. This is the value of brainstorms—and their trap. Everything is dazzling in this planning stage. Every idea evokes a dream or a memory. "And along with the architects," Verda continues, "here and there was a theorist or somebody who had written a book. There was this guy who wrote a seminal book about LA water. Michael... I can't think of his last name, but I have the book, I'll bring it in."

"Mike Davis?"

"Yes! He drove us in a truck through the LA River. He gave us a tour, our own personal tour of the LA River."

It's a moment of inspiration. Mike Davis, despite the unmemorable plainness of his name—no Lebbeus Woods he!—is an iconic chronicler of LA's transformation from a land of orange groves and

F
F
T
T
T

-

01
-
18

76

"Drawing on desert Bedouins, and the plains Indians and herdsmen on the Mongolian steppes George and Nikki pulled the truck free from its 'camper van' inclinations, to a purer, more aesthetically sustainable vision of nomadism."

golden beaches to the urban monster it is today. To have received his personal tour of the LA River, the perfect symbol of that transformation, is like taking a walk around Gettysburg with Shelby Foote. The idea of this team meeting today was to start nailing down some practical options for the truck besides Bakersfield, but Verda's memories of riding down the river with Mike Davis stir new excitement. And new excitement stirs more brainstorming—perhaps the truck could offer its own tours. Perhaps the team could construct a series of mile markers. "I think tours are a great idea," Verda says, "and mile markers, maybe even the mile markers could tell stories. We can come up with specifics. But, yes, definitely, I LOVE the river."

"Okay, so you're going to call Frank Gehry?" Nikki says, and everyone laughs.

Back to the moon.

F
F
T
T

01

18

77

79

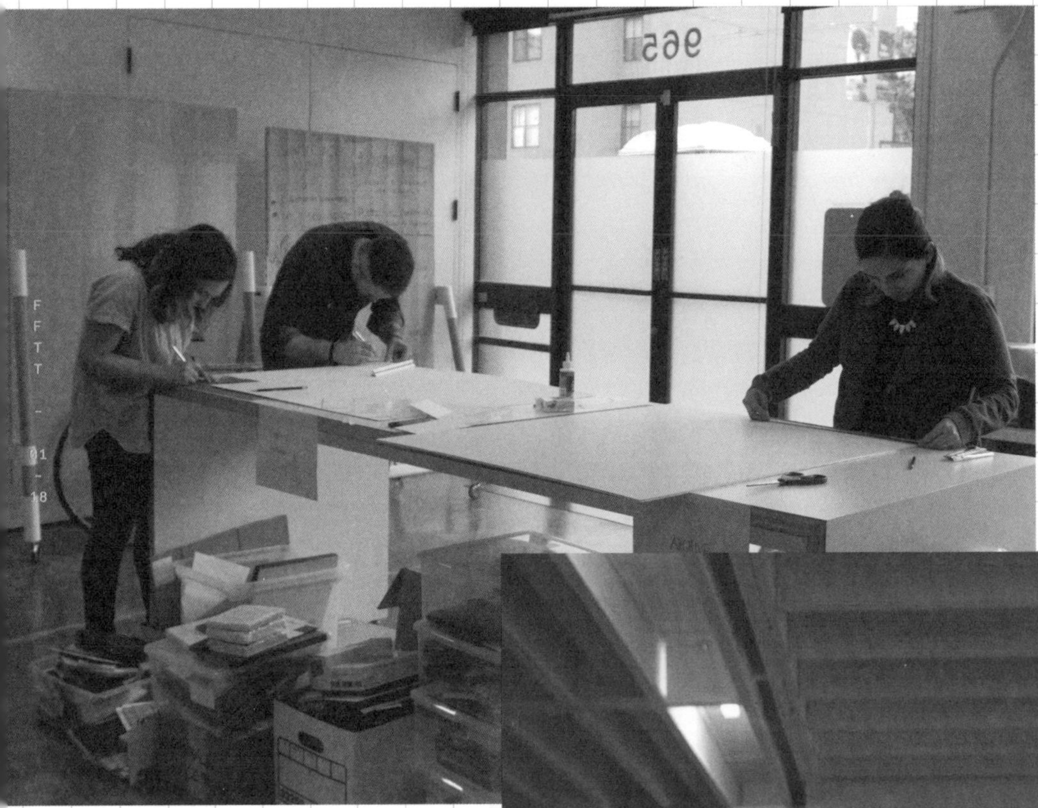

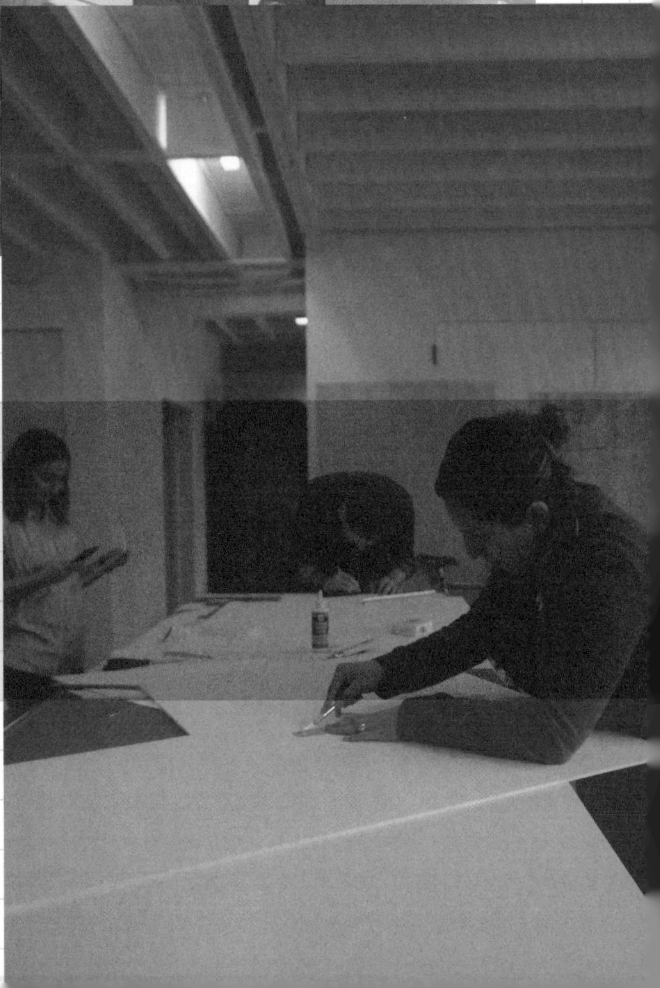

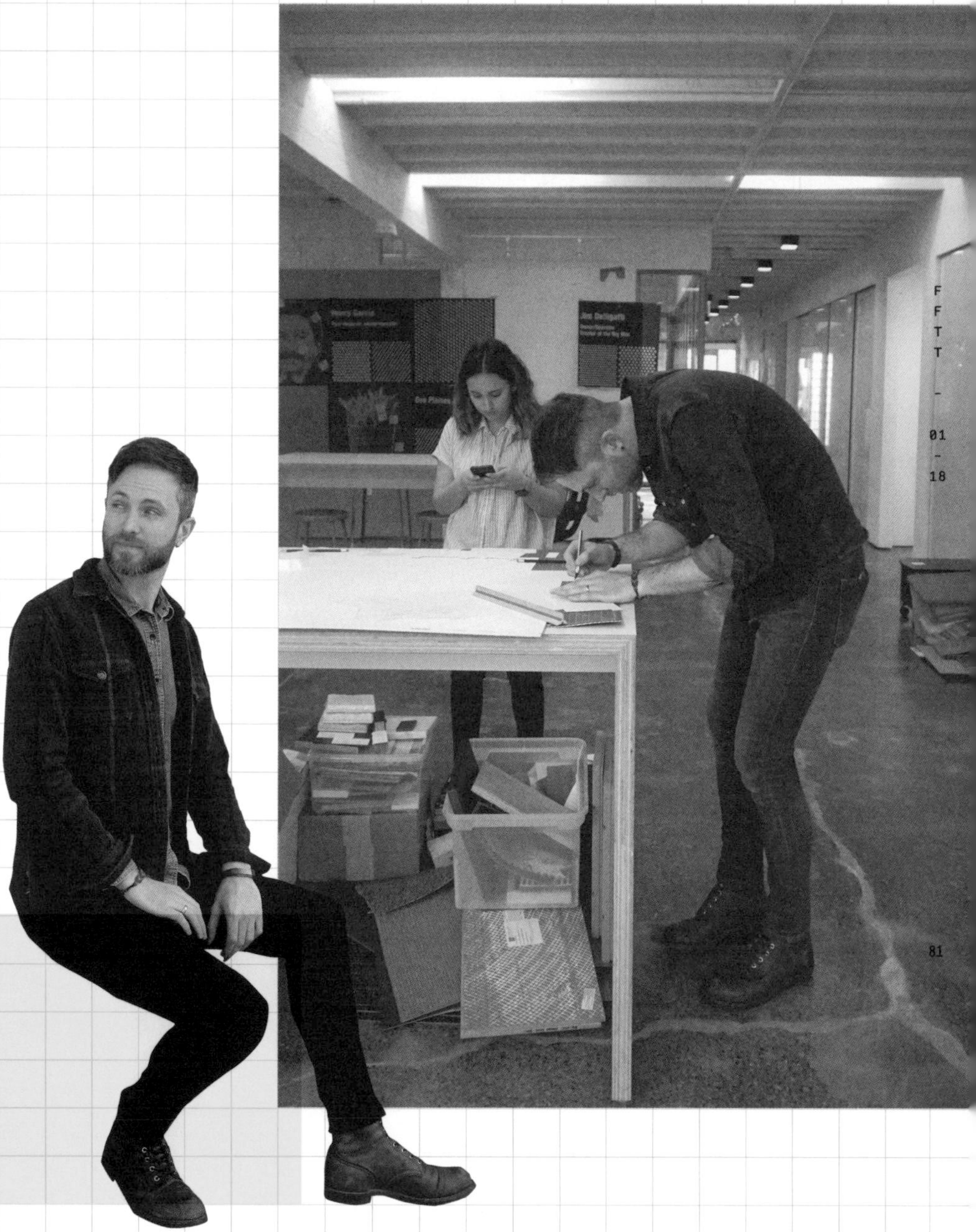

The Fabricator

Learning to live with demolition.
Phil prepares to cut the truck.
Doyle clears the decks.

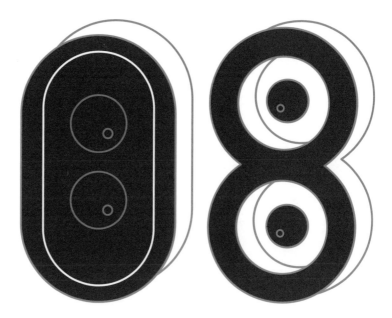

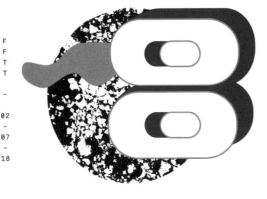

FEBRUARY–JULY 2018

Before the truck can become the Food for Thought Truck it has to be physically transformed. George's sketches, Kristina's sketches, indeed the sketches in everyone's mind, show a cracked-open Fabergé egg sort of vehicle—a strictly no frills, no froufrou, industrial-spirited Fabergé egg to be sure, but the point is its original egg structure will be opened out and augmented. It will remain a truck, yes—someone will have to drive it—but it must be more than that. It must be a functioning design studio. And a stage, potentially. And a video recording booth, potentially. It must unfold to become a plaza many feet wider than its boxy kernel. For any of that to happen someone will have to cut into this metal, attack the structural integrity of this machine and possibly (this is the unspoken fear) turn it into a hunk of junk.

The destruction necessary for repurposing architecture is often shocking to someone outside the industry. Countless episodes of house-flipping shows on HGTV or DIY Network may have mitigated that shock somewhat—most of us now know the mess that must be made before new construction can begin. But it's still a violation of something basic to our sense of propriety to see a sledge-hammer crash into drywall or a crow-bar rip out cabinetry. The fragility of these structures that we perceive as solid is exposed when demo begins. As with the wreckage after an earthquake or a hurricane, our confidence in the wholeness of our world, perhaps even in our own bodily wholeness, is violated when we observe large-scale destruction.

In the case of a truck, there is the additional issue of the gas tank.

The search for a fabricator to make these radical alterations is therefore not a minor matter. George and Kristina meet with an auto-body shop up the street from O+A's office—and get an estimate for the work of $35,000. The figure matches what Chase reckoned it would cost back when the team first discussed the issue, but it's a number to make a project manager choke—way more money than Food for Thought

If buying the truck was O+A's point of no return, Phil Horton's (second from the right) is cutting a hole in its side. Even so, everyone smiles for the camera.

"If a designer were to conjure from his or her imagination a laid-back master craftsman with the soul of an artist, the eye of an architect, the hands of a carpenter and the voice of a late-night FM radio DJ, he or she would summon Phil Horton.

F
F
T
T

-

02

-

07

-

18

Truck could possibly afford. Fortunately Verda has another option in mind.

If a designer were to conjure from his or her imagination a builder and fabricator from the East Bay, a laid-back master craftsman with the soul of an artist, the eye of an architect, the hands of a carpenter and the voice of a late-night FM radio DJ, he or she would summon from some Haight-induced ether Phil Horton from PK Tool and Production. Phil's friendship with Studio O+A goes back to the company's earliest days. He was around for the KODE mobile phone store design back when mobile phones looked like electric shavers. He worked with O+A on some of the firm's first projects with Levi Strauss. "I feel like we've known him almost our entire careers," Verda says. "Family-run business. Philip Horton III. He was always a hands-on fabricator. Always took a lot of care—and truly one of the nicest people I ever met." That counts for a lot in what can be a high-stress business like design. But another bond, surely, is the spirit that comes across when you look at Phil's portfolio: the Tim Burton-inspired Halloween decorations, the stage sets he designed for his daughter Hazel's school plays, the goofy party installations and circus graphics; all of this alongside precision-crafted railings, sculptural doors and windows, hand-made shelves and light fixtures, hand-made signage, hand-made tables. If anyone will grasp the mix of whimsy and pragmatism that Food for Thought Truck represents, Phil Horton is the man.

"Phil was kind enough to sketch up some ideas," George says as he and Phil and Verda meet at the truck in O+A's parking lot late in March. George's own sketches of the truck popping down on one side to form a platform and popping up on the other to form a canopy have guided Phil's drawings on how that might happen from a fabricator's perspective.

He is here because of his long association with O+A —and because his bid has come in under the bid from the guy up the street. Phil is quoting $8,000 for the platform and canopy, with additional fees for interior features as they're selected. But Verda is never done streamlining.

"I had one thought when the price came in at eight grand," she says, hastening to add, "which I think is a fair price…"

But Phil instantly gets the drift. "I can figure out exactly what it's going to cost. There could be ways of shaving it down."

"I don't want you to cut your price or anything. That's not what I'm asking. But it made me think. Could we do what we're trying to do with just one opening? Are we ever going to have both sides open at the same time?"

A pause.

George says, "*Potentially*," drawing out the word to the full length of his reluctance. When a designer has advanced a concept far enough in his mind to have established subconscious parameters around it, any suggestion that upends that concept hits like… well, like a sledgehammer crashing into drywall. "I guess I always envisioned it being in a kind of parking lot scenario as opposed to on a road," George says —meaning his mind's eye vision of the truck opens on two sides.

The discussion moves to what the purpose of the two openings will be: a workshop and stage for the panel that pulls down; a traditional service window for the one that pops up. Everyone stands

over the drawings staring as if the lines on the page are shifting—which they are.

Phil says, "From a cost standpoint I look at it and say, Okay this one's bigger, but it needs to be structurally reinforced and this one's smaller, but there's more detail going on." In other words neither is easy, neither is cheap.

"If we were limited to one side..." George says.

"If we were limited to one side," Verda jumps in, "I would want to figure out how to make this one more flexible. Maybe there's a way to have a smaller window, but then also pop it out and have a bigger opening." To Phil she says, "Why don't you home in on the price a little bit more? Let's start there. And then, George, in the back of your mind be thinking about one opening."

But the back of his mind is already crumbled drywall. George's truck with wings on either side must move forward as a flightless bird.

– – –

Doyle Buddington arrives at the meeting in shorts. Food for Thought Truck's team has come over to Berkeley from San Francisco wearing their jackets as befits an unpredictable day in the breezy, damp Bay Area, but a man as fastidious about design as Doyle Buddington is not going to let a little thing like the weather overrule his judgment of appropriate seasonal attire. And as it turns out, he's right. At Phil Horton's shop where the team has gathered to look at the truck and plan out the millwork, the day turns hot.

Doyle is a partner at Upholstery Workroom in Oakland—and a friend of O+A's since he did the parenthetical sofas arrangement at Artis Ventures in 2014. Verda has chosen him to do the seats in the truck and any other upholstered items the project might need and has asked him to drop by Phil's to take a look at the vehicle and offer advice on the project generally. In his teal golf shirt, khaki shorts, white socks and scholarly spectacles he could be a visiting lepidopterist—Vladimir Nabokov!

Kristina shows him floor plans, sketches and elevations for all the things the team is planning inside the truck: multi-purpose seating, a foldable workshop, pegboard storage, cabinet storage, a tiny kitchen. He listens with his chin in his hand.

"What you're doing is, you're building a boat," he says. "You're trying to cram everything in there—seating, transport, cooking. Kind of using every inch of space." A boat is a happier model than the camper

van George and Nikki were at such pains to avoid a few weeks back, but Doyle's interpretation still seems a bit limiting. Does he not understand the capacity for this vehicle to soar? "Tell me more about the seating," he says.

Kristina explains how the seating is designed to pull out.

"Like a futon?"

"Like a futon, yeah."

"We're trying to figure out if there's a spot for the driver to have a nap," Verda says.

"Well," he pauses, looking into the truck. Sometimes when you have been in a profession for a long time, your judgment acquires the perfect balance of experience, foresight and candor to give you the easy authority of a sage. Doyle Buddington has been in the furniture business for a long time. "My opinion is you're trying to do two things, and you're not going to accomplish either of them well. It's kind of like a sofa bed. It accomplishes two things, but nothing really well. I would say if you stick with the seating, then you can increase your floor space, and if someone's going to lie down they can curl up on it."

"So maybe we work toward making it more comfortable?" Verda says.

"That would be my suggestion."

Kristina seems relieved to be off the hook for designing a fold-out bed. In her sudden release from that chore she mentions possible alternative nap solutions—wall attachments for a hammock, perhaps? Again Doyle expresses his opinion in plain terms:

"You know, the napping part is interesting, but I wonder if it's really going to happen. This is pretty open. If you're in a rural area you might be able to nap in it. In the city it's like..." He grimaces as if to say, You wouldn't catch ME sleeping in the back of a truck! "It's a good concept, and if you had more space you could probably pull it off, but with this you're sacrificing too many things around it to achieve that. You don't have a lot of footprint here."

"So would it be a two-seater?" Verda says.

"It could be a bench seat. That's an option. You'll be able to sit two people—maybe three. But why would three people sit there?" Doyle's profession as an upholsterer is to look at materials in one state—flat fabrics, bare frames—and calculate how they will fold into another. It's a talent that requires anticipating

F
F
T
T

02
–
07
–
18

87

F
F
T
T

02
-
07
-
18

90

problems and seeing things not as they are right now, but as they will be. "You're going to have to take this to the DMV when you're done and get it inspected, right?"

Verda looks sheepish. "I dunno."

"Usually you do. How's the registration?"

"Um. I don't know. Chase knows." Chase is not on hand for the meeting this morning.

"Okay," Doyle says. "Well usually when you do a conversion on a vehicle you have to go to the DMV and get it inspected. Make sure that the lights work —and all of that. That may be an issue if you put seatbelts back here for passengers."

"We wondered how comfortable that would be —riding in the back."

"It would be terrible," Doyle says. "It would be just terrible."

"Would anyone really want to ride back there?"

"No one would."

Doyle's ability to see beyond good intentions to the way things will actually play out hits the project like a brisk wind blowing away everything that isn't nailed down. It's a valuable contribution, but for Food for Thought Truck's team it is also a test of stamina. Can their high hopes withstand this gale of plain talk?

"This floor looks good," he says, perhaps sensing the need for a pause. "This floor is great. Whatever you put on here would work really well."

"Cork?" Verda says.

"I'd stay away from cork." Well that didn't last long. "What I see as happening here is—this truck is going to leak. It's a given. This is going to leak in the rain. If it doesn't leak in the rain it's going to leak when you drive it down the road in the rain. So anything you have in here should be able to withstand a little bit of water." Phil holds his tongue. It is his job to build out the truck so it doesn't leak in the rain. "The other thing is," Doyle continues, "the lighter colors of the cork, are going to pick up…" He enunciates the words like a man picking popcorn out of his teeth. "…ROAD GRIT. Which is what's on here right now." An aside to which Phil, again, resists rebuttal.

A project as dreamy as Food for Thought Truck needs a straight-talking realist like Doyle Buddington to steer it away from missteps—but good Lord! How much realism can a group of young idealists take ?

- - -

Before Phil cuts the hole in the side of the truck he drops by O+A's office to talk about it with the team. "If I have a clear path," he says, "it's not going to take a long time. I don't know which areas I'm going to cut first. It's one of those things where, when you're cutting down a tree you want to approach it from different angles and make sure it doesn't fall the wrong way. I just don't want to cut through anything structural that compromises the integrity of the vehicle. So I might do a little here and a little over there. It's probably way too much caution for what it really is, but it's better to think about it a bit more than just rush through it and all of a sudden you really don't have anything left to work with."

As if to punctuate Phil's point, the sound of a saw ripping through wood drowns out any sharp intakes of breath occasioned by the thought of nothing left to work with. Construction is underway on a building across Tehama Street from O+A's office, and as this discussion is taking place out in the street next to the parked truck, the sound of hammers and saws accompany Phil's hypotheticals with hard notes of actuality.

Phil, Kristina and George launch into a long discussion about the Z extrusions that will secure the plywood platform in the 4 x 8-foot hole he is going to cut—replacing the missing metal with wood. They talk about the hinges Phil will use and the marine-grade finish he will apply to keep the wood from weathering too quickly (and maybe forestall Doyle Buddington's anticipated leaks). Suddenly the pleasure of working in solid forms engulfs the discussion. Breaking free of Ivan Sutherland's virtual world, designers and fabricator come together over thicknesses of plywood and layers of sealant. It is their link to the origins of their trade, doing out here in an alleyway south of Market Street in 2018 what Christopher Wren must have done in alleyways on Ludgate Hill in 1670.

Verda arrives.

"So, Verda," George says, "I guess the decision for next Friday is do we want Phil to cut the hole?" Next Friday O+A has an event planned at which they would like to feature the Food for Thought Truck.

"Ideally we would love to have the hole," Verda says—better to show the truck as a work in progress than as a plain old delivery van. "But if you cut a hole and it's not put back together, can you even drive it?"

"I feel a little more confident than I did a couple of days ago," Phil says, perhaps revealing more about his process than is good for his clients to know. He didn't feel confident a couple of days ago? "I can definitely cut the hole. I don't know that I'll get much further than that." He means he can cut the hole by Friday, but he won't be able to attach the platform that will seal it back up. Even so: "I'm not worried about driving it back here with the opening. I'll drive it around the block two or three times and if it feels like there's something dangerous about it, I'll shore it up with something inside, plywood or something. We'll make it work. I've done stranger things."

Before the meeting breaks up it is decided that if Phil can cut the hole on Thursday, Chase—who lives not far away—will pick it up at Phil's shop on Friday morning and drive it to work in advance of the evening's event. Chase is not around to agree to this arrangement, but the team seems confident that he too has done stranger things.

A few days later having studied and measured and measured again, having crawled over every inch of the truck to satisfy himself that he knows what he's doing, Phil puts on his goggles, and into the quiet of keep-it-mellow Berkeley introduces the shriek of a reciprocating saw penetrating metal— Food for Thought Truck's metal!

F
F
T
T
–
02
–
07
–
18

91

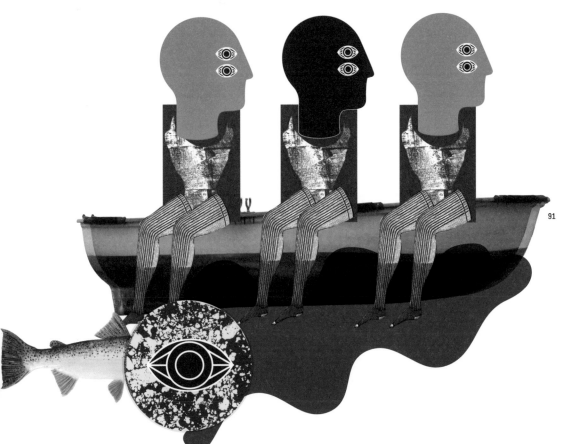

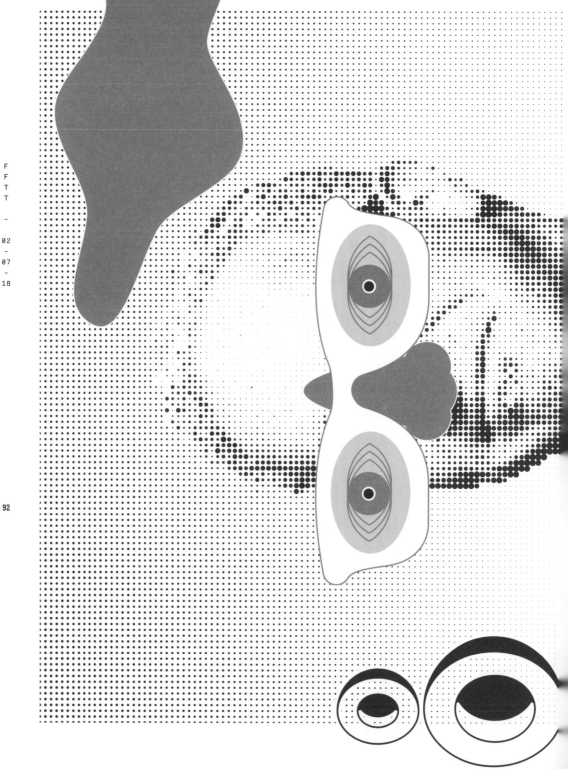

F
F
T
T
-
02
-
07
-
18

94

Doyle Buddington's years
in the furniture business
have given him keen instincts
into how much 'design'
a small space can handle.

95

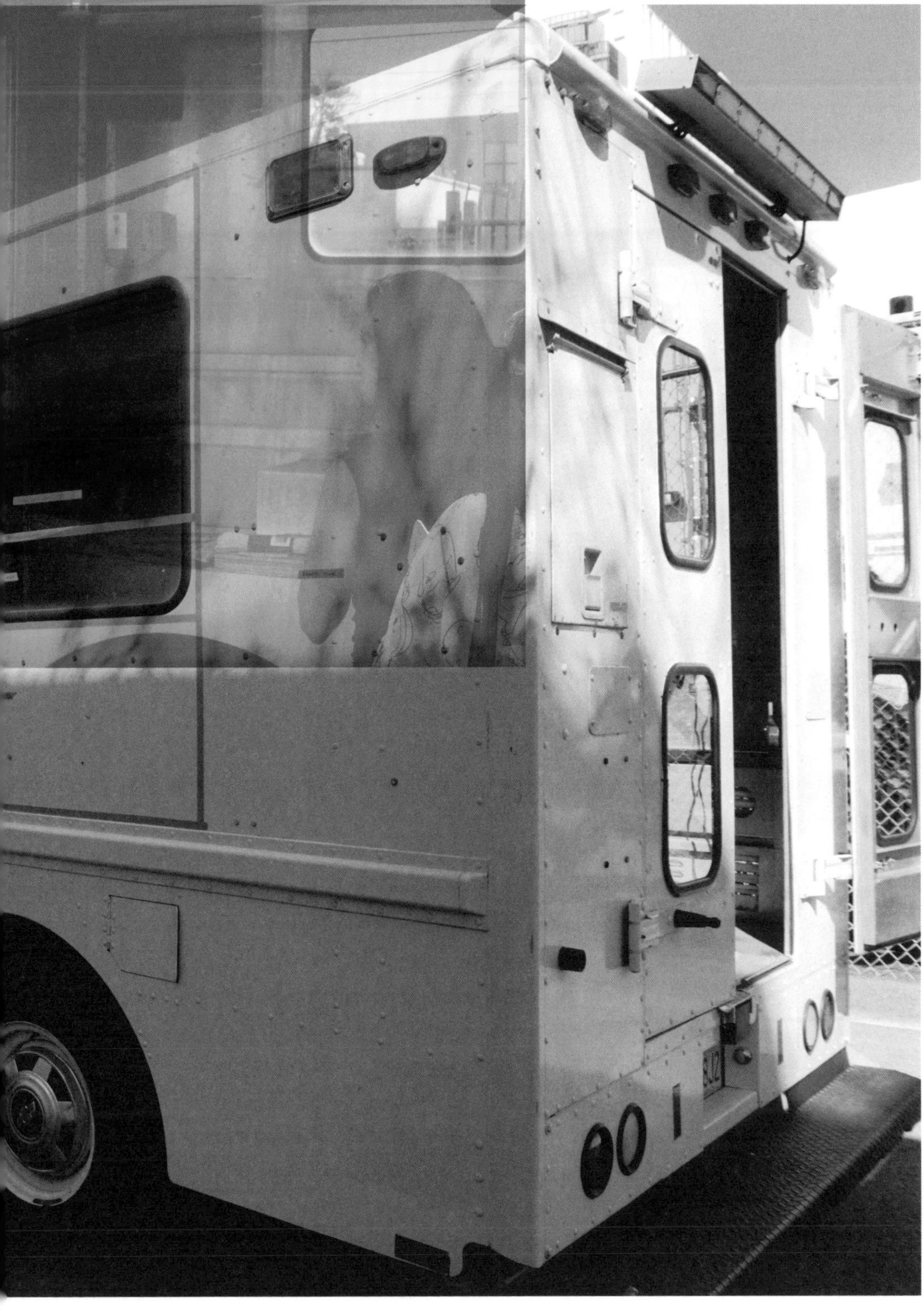

F
F
T
T
-
02
-
07
-
18

F
F
T
T

–

17

–

18

–

19

98

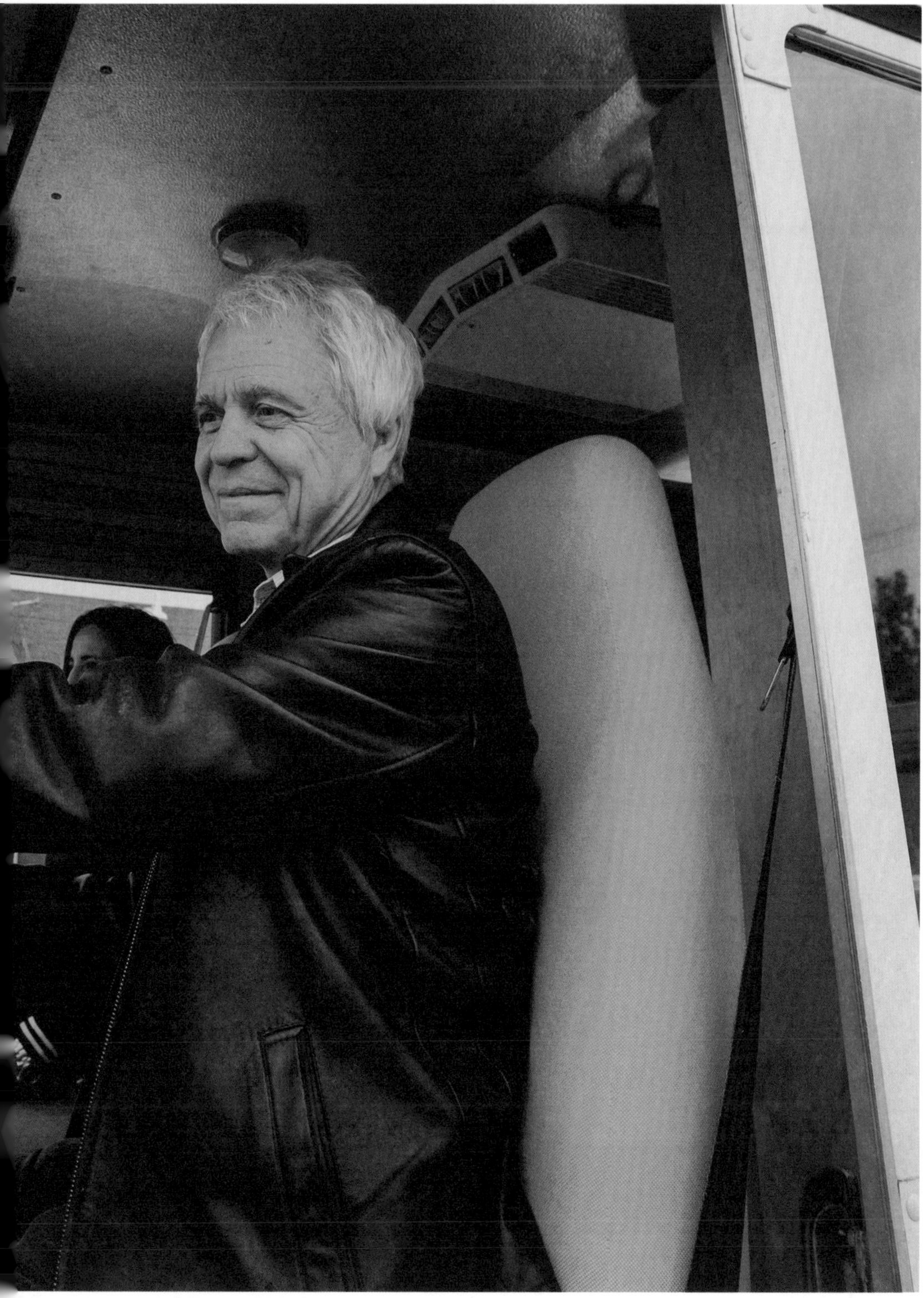

"'To finish first, you must first finish.'"

Rick Mears
Race Car Drive

Imagine
Eastchester

"'I'
to
at b
a hu
being

ana Lily Amirpo...
Film Director

"Lay in the weeds and wait, and when you get your chance to say something, say something good."

Merle Haggard
Musician

F
F
T
T

–

17
–
18
–
19

F
F
T
T

–

17
–
18
–
19

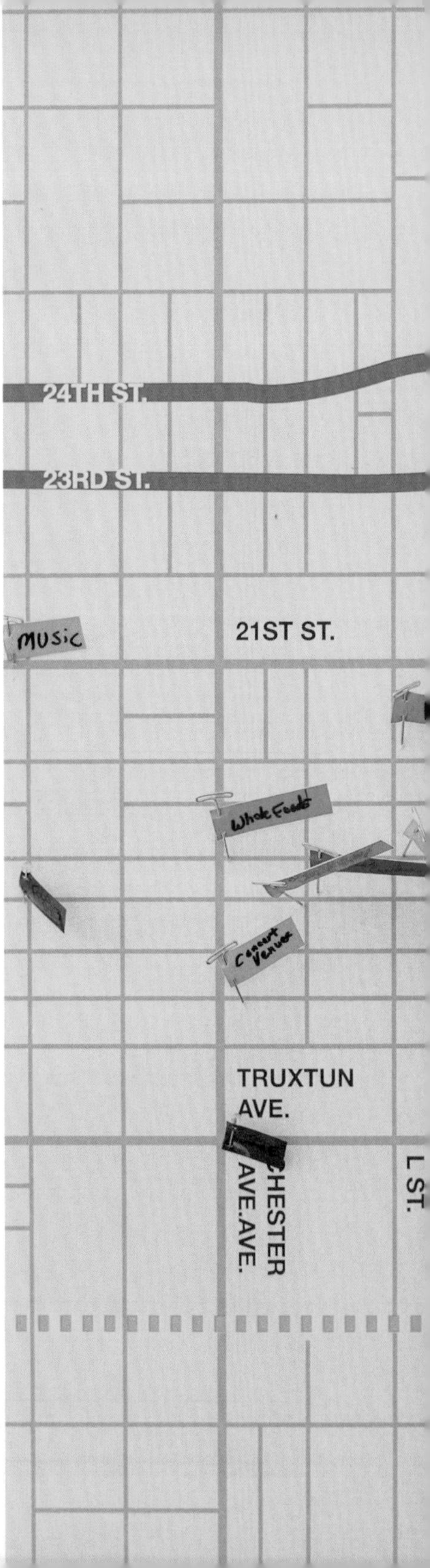

24TH ST.

23RD ST.

21ST ST.

MUSiC

Whole Foods

Concert Venue

TRUXTUN AVE.

CHESTER AVE. AVE.

L ST.

F
F
T
T
–
17
–
18
–
19

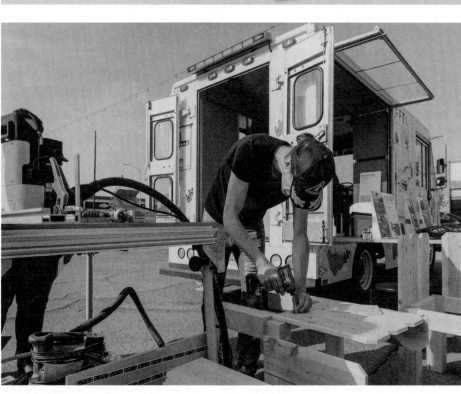

F
F
T
T

–

17

–

18

–

19

YOU ARE
0.2 MILES
FROM THE
LA RIVER

ourriverla oa_fftt   RIVER LA   FFTt FOOD FOR THOUGHT TRUCK

F
F
T
T

–

17

–

18

–

19

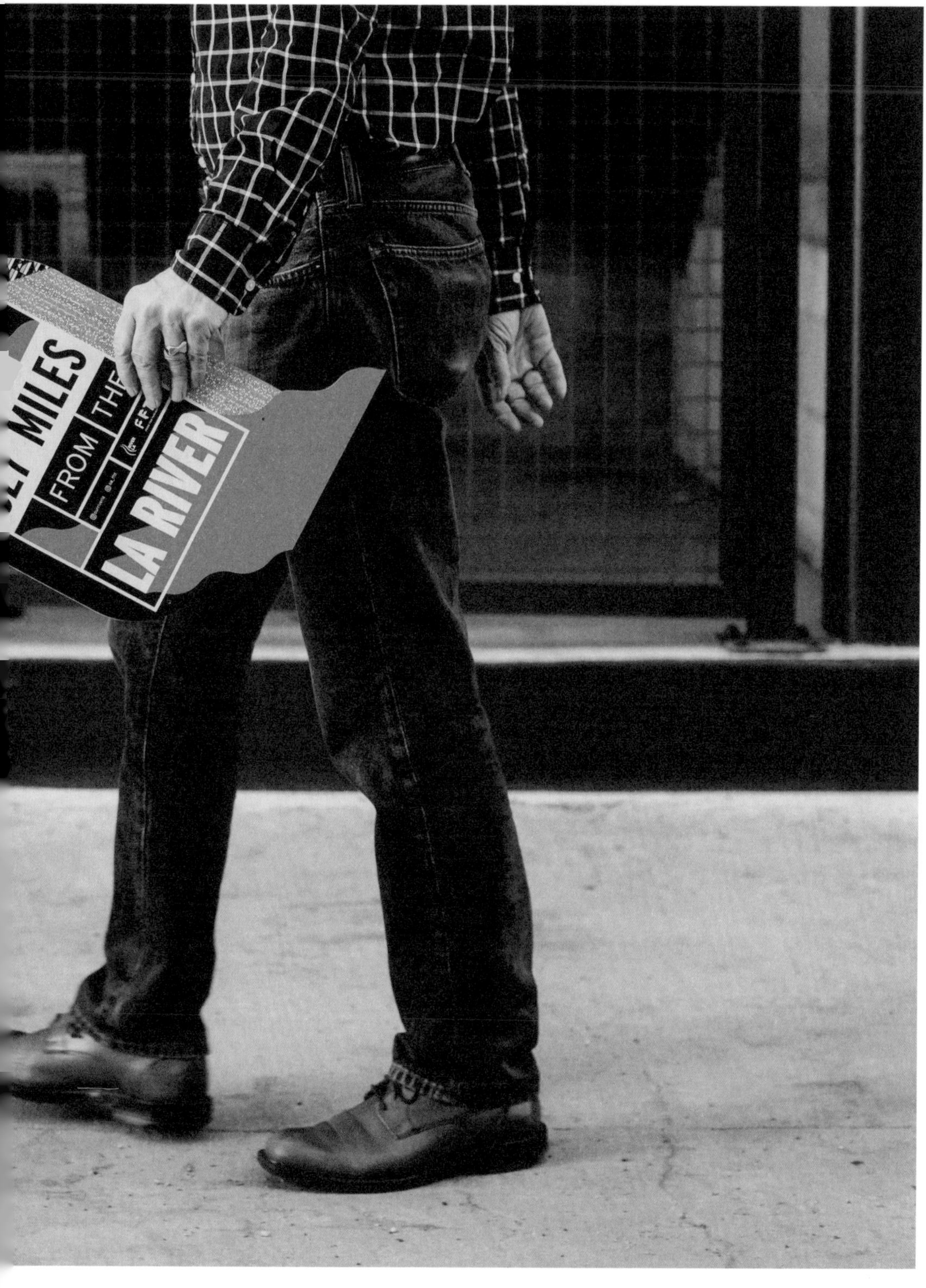
MILES
FROM
LA RIVER

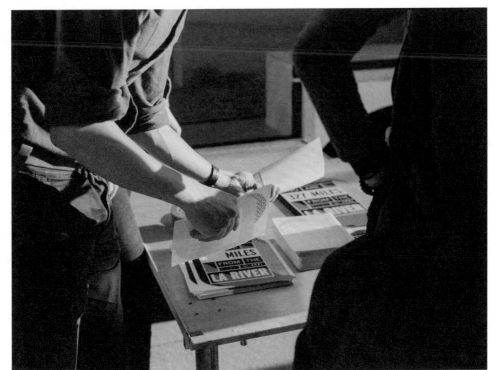

F
F
T
T
-
17
-
18
-
19

The Preview

Steering into headwinds.
Studio or soothsayer?
A festival of dreamers falls for the truck.

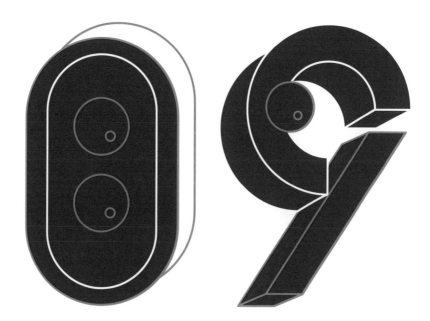

JUNE 2018

When the Transamerica Pyramid debuted in 1972, the *San Francisco Chronicle* called it "an abomination." *The Washington Post* settled for "hideous nonsense." When the Loma Prieta earthquake wrecked the Embarcadero Freeway in 1989, tearing down the crippled structure and building a new waterfront turned into a battle—a large contingent of city leaders wanted the freeway (and the status quo) repaired. When Herzog and De Meuron's new MH de Young Museum replaced another casualty of the same earthquake in Golden Gate Park, the result was widely judged a masterpiece, but it could not escape trolling on social media: "The 2nd Ugliest Building in San Francisco," one angry Yelper wrote in 2011.

Even in a city famous for alternative lifestyles, architectural alternatives have often been hard-won. Indeed, for many years, San Francisco was known as a center of radical social and political thinking with a culturally conservative resistance to anything that might mess up the view. Beatniks, hippies, gay rights pioneers all launched their revolutions from cozy Victorians on streets that hadn't changed much since the early 1900s.

San Francisco's emergence in the last 20 years as one of the world's pre-eminent 'design cities' comes therefore as an unexpected twist. Part of it can be attributed to the cultural spin-off from those early upheavals—Robert Crumb peddling *ZAP Comix* from a baby carriage on Haight Street in the 1960s; Gilbert Baker sewing up the first rainbow flag for the Gay Freedom Day Parade in 1978. But a large measure of the city's flowering as a design hub must be credited to its latest wave of radical thinkers: the techies. To be specific this revolution broke first in Silicon Valley, not in San Francisco, but because it was nothing less than a wholesale reimagining of the way virtually everything in modern life was done, its impact spread like an earthquake's shocks.

When Studio O+A opened its doors as a two-person space planning operation in Fremont, California in 1991 it was entering the field of workplace design at

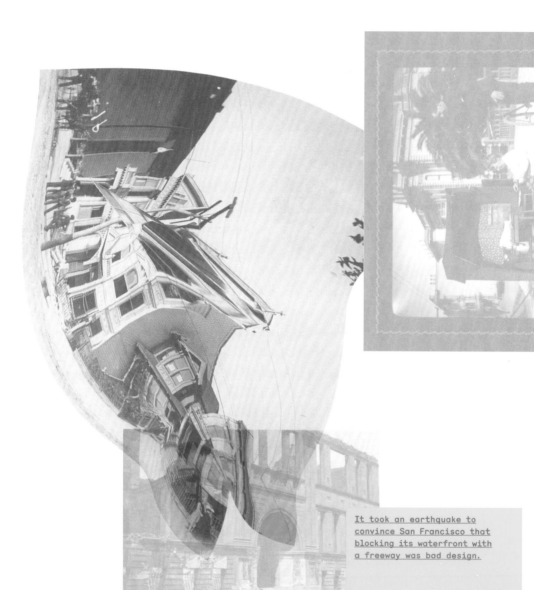

FFTT - 06 - 18

131

It took an earthquake to convince San Francisco that blocking its waterfront with a freeway was bad design.

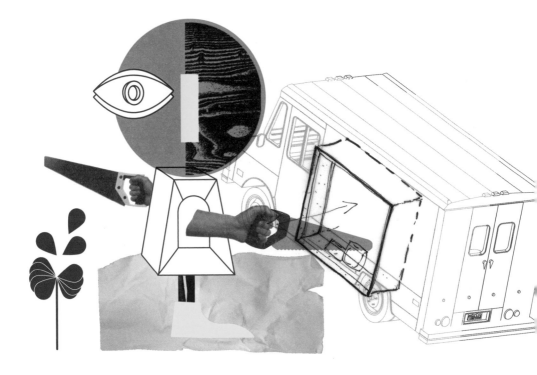

precisely the moment when tech companies were questioning the basic protocols of work. One reason companies like O+A and Clive Wilkinson Architects (which also started in 1991 in Los Angeles) gained ground quickly on established firms like Gensler and HOK is that they were working with clients who were disrupting design conventions as profoundly as they were disrupting their own industries. The resulting culture of change made California generally and the Bay Area specifically a hotbed of new design thinking.

Which is why when San Francisco Design Week rolls around in June of 2018, O+A is eager to host. This annual celebration of the city's design community is managed by the local chapter of AIGA, the professional association for graphic designers, but it has long included architects, interior designers and product designers. One of Design Week's featured events—the Studio Crawl where guests visit the offices and studios of design firms around the city—is a great way to showcase new work, to recruit new talent and generally to catch up with others in the industry. For Food for Thought Truck it's a chance to preview a project in progress and get feedback on ideas that continue to evolve. The team is excited about giving the truck a Studio Crawl sneak preview—but one question nags at everyone. Will Phil have it in presentable shape in time for the show?

- - -

"Wow! That's a big hole."

On the Thursday night before Friday's Studio Crawl Chase goes to Phil's Berkeley shop to pick up the truck. While Chase was a key player in Food for Thought Truck's early stages—researching vehicle options, helping with the selection, overseeing the inspection and tune-up—the crush of his workload on commercial projects has kept him removed from the day-to-day of the truck's progress. He isn't up to date on where the design is heading, hasn't seen any recent drawings, doesn't know what to expect.

Chase's girlfriend Danielle Pepi drives him to Phil's place, and as they get out of the car, they see the truck waiting in the parking lot like a good friend after a really bad week. Wow. Like the gap a lost tooth leaves, the hole in the side of the truck seems larger than what was there before. It's as if one whole side of the vehicle has been yanked out. Phil will put it back, of course. The gap will be filled with a handsome

two-piece implant—a canopy that flips up, a platform that pulls down—but right now the truck that Chase collected in good condition from Alex Nerguizian six months ago looks pretty banged up.

None of which gets mentioned in the quick and friendly transfer of keys.

Chase and Danielle live in Oakland, about 15 minutes from Phil's shop—too short a distance to get a good feel for how the truck will handle on the bridge tomorrow, especially since they stop at a café on the way home. Chase drives the truck; Danielle drives the car. "I park the truck out front where I can keep an eye on it," Chase recalls later, "and people are staring like—What the hell is this?" The East Bay sees its share of beat vehicles, but this truck with one side blown out is a head-turner even here. As Chase watches from the café, a couple of kids climb into the open cavity—well, why not? It can't possibly be a serious motor vehicle. Surely it's some kind of playground installation. Their parents call them back.

Back home after the café stop, Chase parks in front of his house. He and Danielle bring inside for safekeeping everything in the truck that could conceivably be stolen. It feels weird to leave a vehicle wide open on a city street overnight, but it's not likely anyone would bother to hot-wire a truck so badly damaged or so easy to identify. Sure enough, in the morning Food for Thought Truck is right where they left it after what appears to be an uneventful night. No graffiti on the truck. No one sleeping inside.

The drive from Oakland to San Francisco echoes Chase's earlier drive from Alex Nerguizian's house back in January—but it's a ghostly echo. Back then Marbel rode along shooting video of the sparkling day and the smooth bridge crossing; Men Without Hats pulsated on the radio while Chase moved his shoulders in time to the music and Marbel giggled behind the camera. Today Chase drives alone and the only music is the roar of commuter traffic blasting through that giant hole. Wind blasts too, a steady thundering riptide of wind. Chase has rolled down the front windows to let the air flow. The result is a tempestuous, ear-battering gale, but his shoulders are squared this time and he is leaning forward—as if body language could keep the truck from tipping over. It's a serious worry. Such accidents have occurred on the bridge with trucks that didn't have a wind-collecting hole in their sides. With relief then

F
F
T
T

-

06

-

18

Tag Us! #foodforthoughttruck #oplusa

CALIFORNIA

FOOD FOR THOUGHT TRUCK

SF DESIGN WEEK
06.08.2018

Design is an aggressively social profession. Perhaps because designers spend the heart of every day solo, wrestling lines and shapes on a screen, they never miss an opportunity to meet, to schmooze, to step out for coffee, to go to (or host) a party. It's a culture O+A has always embraced.

F
F
T
T

-

06
-
18

(driving this truck seems always to be an exercise in relief), Chase heads down the off-ramp into San Francisco.

"Any squatters?" George asks when the truck is safely parked at O+A.

The staff have come out to inspect the damage. "It's a bigger cut than I was expecting," Al says.

"Go big or go home," George counters.

Nikki runs her fingertips along the edge of the opening. "It's a pretty clean cut. I was expecting it to be all jagged." It's as if she is trying to convince herself.

Whatever their private reservations, there's no time to fret about them. This roughed-up, lost-toothed version of the vehicle has to greet guests in a couple of hours. The team sets about getting it dressed for the party. George and Nikki string fairground lights across the parking lot. Marbel decorates the interior walls with some of the project's early sketches. Someone scavenges carpet samples to lay down a passable floor. Someone else brings out an Adirondack chair and three neon orange stools to make the bare space more inviting. Verda tapes a large map of California to the truck's exterior. Liliana Lewicka, O+A's office manager, spreads out copies of *Metropolis Magazine*. It's a rush job, to be sure, but because Food for Thought Truck is an idea first and a truck second, it might be just enough. Changing into their Food for Thought Truck T-shirts, the team anxiously awaits San Francisco Design Week 2018's first Studio Crawlers.

Design is an aggressively social profession. Perhaps because designers spend the heart of every day wrestling lines and shapes on a screen, they never miss an opportunity to meet, to schmooze, to step out for coffee, to go to (or host) a party. It's a culture O+A has always embraced. Primo and Verda travel the world attending design events, speaking, teaching, connecting with colleagues. O+A's office buzzes every day—the staff are forever being called downstairs for a champagne toast to a new client acquired or an old project finished. Staffers bring their dogs to work and their babies and their parents. At any given hour, as designers sit hunched in front of their CAD drawings, a contingent of visitors from Japan or Germany or the East Coast may pass through snapping photos. And parties! To work at O+A means an upfront commitment to Valentine's Day and Halloween, ski weekends at Tahoe, sailing on the Bay, film festival after-parties—O+A is not a wallflower firm. So when the first guests trickle in, as the Studio Crawl gets underway, whatever pre-event jitters may have troubled the Food for Thought Truckers quickly disperse. This is something they know how to do.

At some point in the chit-chat they inevitably get around to, "You know as you continue fitting out the truck, keep in mind...", this weave, this tile, this great little customizable bench.

At least they understand the truck isn't finished. Some Studio Crawlers assume this bare bones van with the gaping hole and carpet sample floor is the Food for Thought Truck complete. Neo-Minimalism or something—in design you can never be sure. Even so, they're impressed! So powerful is the gravitational pull of goodwill around this project, so ardently do people want it to be wonderful, that they let their aspirations overrule their eyes. "Even I thought that was it," Lisa says of the makeshift decor—and follows that confession with her *Oh my Gawd!* face.

Gradually, however, as evening falls and gusts of wind catch the fairground lights, a world of alternative possibility takes shape. Something about this rippling light, this agitated air, encourages guests to open their minds. Not since the Food for Thought Truck team first gathered around Verda's map of the US has the project's power to change lives felt so close to the surface. The raw truck with its gaping wound is like one of those ancient oracles that takes the shape of its perceiver's secrets. Studio Crawlers peer into the truck and see their individual hopes for the world.

"This would be so great in my country," a woman from South Africa says. "In South Africa the cities are divided because of apartheid. There's the core city and then there are the townships all around and there are so few services in the townships. A truck that could drive around from place to place and bring planning to these areas… that would be so great."

A man marching forward into O+A's office calls out as he passes, "IS IT GOING TO BE SOLAR?" He does not break stride, but his booming voice makes clear he assumes it will be SOLAR.

Liliana sits in the truck with a group from ALL Power Labs, a Berkeley nonprofit dedicated to promoting gasification. That's the process of turning biomass into fuel for internal combustion engines—a technique that dates back to World War II. The conversation in the truck is all about how the time may be right, given the climate crisis, the energy crisis and the world garbage crisis, to bring this proven technology back on a global scale. "Maybe Verda would be interested in running this truck on trash," Liliana says.

A young married couple—architects both—stop at the truck and imagine where they would drive it. To her grandmother's town in rural Mississippi— what a feast of projects they could dream up for it there! They are bursting with questions about the logistics—how far will it go? How many will go with it? Will they sleep in the truck? Could they take it to Mississippi? For a moment it's a summer evening in the South, crickets humming, lightning bugs blinking, someone's blue-tick hound asleep on the porch and parked out front: Food for Thought Truck, glowing like a sharecropper's shack and rocking with fiddle music…

Quite a few of the Studio Crawlers this evening are design students. This truck is an embodiment of why many of them entered the field in the first place—to do good things for the world, to make spaces that make a difference in people's lives. It's a measure of how the profession has changed that what was once a career in creating plush homes for the wealthy, or high-concept decor for fancy retail stores and restaurants, is now just as likely to be a career in imagining affordable housing for low-income people, or work environments that stimulate creativity, or urban spaces that mitigate climate change impacts, or indoor/outdoor interfaces that literally bring sunshine into people's lives. Somehow in the last 20 years design has become a moral profession. "These folks are just out of school," George says of the youngest Studio Crawlers. "They've just finished designing projects like this for their classes and suddenly—here it is!" What better validation than to see your personal aesthetic made real? It's an affirmation that you made the right choice, that your dream career is doable, that your parents will be proud.

No surprise then that the selfie station is busy all night. (The masking tape + is your best place to stand.) All kinds of people, not just students, want to get their pictures taken with the truck. They all want to pose next to hope, next to optimism. They all want to join a team, any team that is going to make things better. When a group of students climb into the truck for a long gab-fest it's like they're climbing into their own sketchbooks. It's like an animated movie where real people step into a chalk-and-pencil truck and chug off down the road in search of new adventures. A classmate comes up and points his camera at them. The girl sitting on the bench that covers the wheel well turns and throws out her arms as if to embrace him. Or is it this wonderful world she wants to hug?

The Look

The team picks a palette.
Brand as wordplay and as science.
Paulina recites her alphabet.

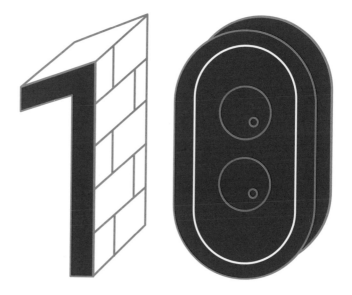

140

[Softly] "Hand-crafted. Honest."

[More softly] "Intriguing."

[So softly you can hardly hear] "Curious."

"Wait. What did you say?"

Nikki speaks up in a more confident voice: "Oh, I said hand-crafted or honest."

Kristina also speaks up. "I feel like curious is better than unassuming."

Nikki says, "Do you like mysterious?"

Unlikely as it seems, they are choosing a color palette for the truck. Perhaps because it does seem unlikely they deliver their initial suggestions in near-whispers, like shy children in class uncertain of the lesson. Only when challenged by Verda—"Wait. What did you say?"—does personal pride prod them to raise their voices.

Verda is writing their words on the wall. Nikki, Kristina, George, Al, Marbel and O+A graphic artist Paulina McFarland are seated at the conference table, playing along at this point, though it seems no one is quite sure how this competitive wordplay is going to lead to a particular shade of green.

"Okay, NOW," Verda says circling three words —Collaborative, Adventurous, Mysterious—"now we have to come up with…"

"The color of Mysterious."

"Exactly."

One of design's bedrock functions is to build a framework of meaning around choices that non-designers make instinctively (or indifferently)—in effect to ascribe a purpose to green. Though the truck as currently envisioned will be stripped down and utilitarian, color will still be an element in the upholstery, the furniture and the system graphics that will brand the project.

Today Verda and the team are trying to impose some order on the way they choose their palette. Color is such an emotion-charged element, it arouses such passions that picking colors for a project can be a contentious process. "I love this bright yellow!" one designer will say, while behind her another is crossing her eyes. Verda's aim is to rein in this fervor by beginning with words.

F
F
T
T

—

06
—
07
—
18

Colors and textures
are the parts of
a design
most subliminally
felt and most
consciously chosen.

141

> "**Whether you get there via witchcraft or environmental psychology, 'the look' is almost always the thing that endures.**"

What words does Food for Thought Truck evoke? What colors do those words suggest? It's an approach in keeping with O+A's tradition of building a design through narrative. What better discipline for a euphoric eye than this harness of words?

"Okay," Verda says. "Are we happy with these?"

"Well, we're definitely Collaborative," Nikki says.

George agrees. "Collaborative and Adventurous. Not sure I get Mysterious."

"Under cover," Verda suggests. "Camouflaged. What is this mysterious truck in town?"

Behind her Al crosses his eyes.

"I like these" Kristina says, leaning over a table of color swatches. "I like them because they aren't bright, but they have a sense of..."

"Wait!" Verda says. "You're jumping ahead. You're not supposed to look at the colors before we settle on the words!"

Is there an element of Harry Potter here? Unruly young wizards recklessly trying out their spells? Now that the class understands the game, all reticence flies out the window. Everyone talks at once, shouting out words that might supplant Collaborative, Adventurous, Mysterious. Verda's marker skids across the wall.

She stops, looks at the list of words she has written. "We should narrow this down." She turns to her class of wizards, stricken. "We have too many up here!"

Beginning with words is supposed to be a reductive exercise—eliminating what doesn't apply until you are left with the words and feelings that match most closely the spirit of your project. So if Food for Thought Truck is Mysterious what combination of inky indigos, shadowed greens and foggy grays capture that word in a designer's mind? Restricting the palette to those colors that can be reasonably matched with Collaborative, Adventurous, Mysterious (or whatever else they choose) gives the designers a welcome structure. They don't have to pick from an infinite color wheel. There's a fence around their playground.

Eventually, after more shouts and debate and lexical roughhousing, the young wizards return to their original three words. The time has come, finally, to put down the dictionary and look at some colors. Like children unleashed in a candy factory they crowd around the table on which Verda has assembled some options. Now they will have to eliminate those they cannot apply to one of their three words and choose favorites from those that remain. There is a pause as the spectrum dislodges its usual tumble of emotions.

"I hate all of these," Paulina says.

- - -

Later in the summer at a Workbench presentation at O+A environmental psychologist Sally Augustin gives a talk to the firm's staff about the scientific underpinnings of what they do. Augustin's organization is Design with Science, a consulting firm that offers insights from cognitive research to aid designers in making decisions. You could say it's the scientific approach to what Verda and team attempted to do with witchcraft.

"Brains is brains," Sally Augustin begins. Her point is that the way we experience space seems to be hardwired and that designers creating spaces for people should be aware of some basic cognitive realities. For example, on privacy, a subject of great interest to O+A's workplace creators, Augustin cites research that when 70 percent of a church's pews are full, congregants split off and form another church. In situations where people are under more or less constant scrutiny, she says—prisons or big companies with large open-plan workplaces—they tend to seek solitude in bathroom stalls.

As Augustin continues her talk, citing this or that study that extroverts like art with people in it, while introverts prefer landscapes; this or that research that seeing the color red degrades analytical performance, while seeing the color green promotes creativity—as she expounds on these findings a larger theme emerges. It's the theme that O+A has been promoting almost from its earliest days and the theme that Food for Thought Truck will test again next month.

Design matters. Design has an impact for good or ill. It is not a transaction of fashion or trend—or rather it is not only that. Everyone's response to design is built into his or her biology; it is part of the fundamental process of cognition. The people who make design a profession, therefore, have a responsibility to create spaces that have impacts beneficial to an individual's and a society's betterment. They have a responsibility to observe the consequences of what they're doing and to let those consequences inform the next design.

Food for Thought Truck is about to move off the worktable and into the streets. As Sally Augustin speaks, the stakes of that move come into focus. The impact of this project will depend on the skills of the team, the receptivity of their partners and the dimensions of the task, but it will also depend (it's humbling to know) on reflexes built into our very cells.

– – –

Whether you get there via witchcraft or environmental psychology, 'the look' is almost always the thing that endures. It's a common observation that George Cruikshank had as much to do with the way generations of readers imagined Charles Dickens' world as the author had. Cruikshank was Dickens' friend and illustrator and his quirky renditions of Victorian England came to be everyone's mental image of that time and place—to Dickens' everlasting benefit.

To test the truth of this claim consider an author of similar stature writing at about the same time—Fyodor Dostoevsky. His characters are just as vivid and his stories even wilder than Dickens' are, but because Dostoevsky had no Russian Cruikshank, his fictional world does not exist as a distinct visual presence to modern readers in the way Dickens' world does. Movies made from Dostoevsky's work have been less frequent and less successful than the many Dickens adaptations and his name has not become a common adjective. Professors of Russian literature understand what 'Dostoevskyan' suggests, but everyone who reads or sees movies or attends a Christmas fair knows what 'Dickensian' means.

All of which explains why, as the summer progresses, Food for Thought Truck turns to Paulina McFarland. Paulina is this project's Cruikshank, the senior O+A graphic designer chosen to create a visual vocabulary for the truck. Paulina came to San Francisco from Chicago, and to Chicago from Poland, and the wit of her art, the sureness of her original eye, seem directly descended from the startling imagery of the Polish School of Posters. (When Paulina's turn came to helm a weekly staff

meeting at O+A, her personal presentation—with which all employees are expected to end their meeting—was an introduction to that world-renowned art movement. The posters she projected on that Monday morning—at once comic, macabre, erotic and political—were a bit more provocative than the staff meeting's usual fare of vacation snapshots or favorite interiors.)

Paulina, then, is ideally suited to capture the quirky personality of a still-metamorphosing Food for Thought Truck. As a graphic designer she has a reputation for abundance. If she is to present options at a design development meeting she will cover the table with sketches, often drawn from three or four separate concepts. "It's essentially a personality flaw," she says. "Very hard for me to settle on something unless I'm absolutely sure that it's the right thing. I explore every possible option. Every blog on how to be a successful designer says, 'Show the client three options. Don't show them five. Don't show them ten. You're going to overwhelm them.' I've made it work for me somehow."

Which is not to say the process is painless. Reviewing logos with Verda one afternoon, Paulina spreads out at least ten options, probably more. Verda moves around the conference table with her arms folded. Her placeholder comment in these situations is usually, "Hm." There are lots of 'Hm's' today and lots of long silences. Pretty nerve-wracking when it's your work under review—Paulina stands by saying little. Verda leans over a logo that reduces Food for Thought Truck to a somewhat abstract FFTT.

"Where's the other F?" Verda says.

"Well it's not an obvious one," Paulina says. Some of her other logos are straightforward and easy to read, but on this one she has been a little playful.

"I see two T's and an F," Verda says.

Paulina traces the hidden F with her finger. "You have the F in this shape too."

"Oh, it's F in both directions."

"It's a little bit more abstract, but if you look at it you can see two T's and two F's."

"I definitely saw two T's and one F," Verda says, "but the other F is upside down."

There is another long silence. Verda moves around the table. "Hm."

F
F
T
T

–

06
–
07
–
18

143

F
F
T
T

-

06
-
07
-
18

144

"Hey George, good
morning... We had a
robbery here a few days
ago at the warehouse,
van stolen, lots of
tools and equipment."

F
F
T
T

-

06
-
07
-
18

The upshot is that none of the many logos Paulina has proposed today quite hit the mark, and so she must cook up a whole new batch. At the same time the system graphics she designed to be used in Food for Thought Truck's marketing and collateral materials—postcards, T-shirts, stickers, the book—suddenly feel too basic. Her original road trip concept seems right thematically, but the symbols themselves—the road signs and directional signals, the picnic tables, the knife and fork—need more character. "They remind me of school," Verda says. "Signs you would see at school. Symbols you would see for kids. Like this pencil. They seem too simple."

It's exhausting to try again when you think you have emptied the barrel to its dregs, but Paulina—after a weekend of thinking about Food for Thought Truck from different angles—experiences a breakthrough and comes back the next week with a whole new vineyard. "It wasn't quite right," she says later. "Sometimes you have to face that. You think about the totality of the project and it's just not special enough. Or it's missing something. And so we found ourselves in that situation where we had this interesting concept, but it didn't feel like it was O+A. It didn't have the spirit. So I went back to the drawing board, but this time knowing the elements that worked, and it just became pure joy." She taps the new set of images on the table. "This feels good now."

What Paulina has done with her earlier icons is put them through a kind of Polish School of Posters transformation. She has given them a dream life. Her O+A O has become a Slinky, a caterpillar of O's spilling forward. The tines of her fork now bend backwards and her 'too simple' pencil is grasped by a hand that might morph at any moment into a hanging sloth. She has added anatomical icons: a phrenologist's head with facial features stacked vertically as in a Picasso portrait and a series of looking-straight-at-you eyes. She has dreamed up

146

wavy strips of bacon and wavy spoons to go with them. And she has built a visual system of architectural symbols altered by a gravity-defying dream logic—brick walls with one brick floating free, stairs that go nowhere, plinths in eerie pairs. Her piece de resistance is a full alphabet, A to Z, with each letter reimagined as a magical structure. It's a perfect visualization of the Food for Thought Truck spirit—a humble truck turned by dreams into something heroic, something... what were those words from the color selection game?

Collaborative, Adventurous, Mysterious.

At the follow-up meeting where Paulina presents her new designs there are no long silences and no cryptic 'Hm's.' Verda speaks for the team:

"These are awesome!"

- - -

One afternoon in July—a setback: George writes to Phil Horton to check on his progress and receives in reply the following text:

Hey George, good morning. We had a robbery here a few days ago at the warehouse, van stolen, lots of tools and equipment. I've had to spend time filing reports and shopping for replacement tools.

For a few seconds George has to catch his breath. *The truck has been stolen?* All those months of work and thought and hope and yeah, expense—gone in a blink? Then he realizes Phil means his own service van. It wouldn't be accurate to describe George's next thought as relief. Phil has lost a lifetime's collection of tools, the tools he uses to make his living! George wouldn't wish that on anybody. Still, it's human nature when misfortune ruffles your hair on its way to landing on someone else to cling gratefully to your luck. George texts back:"

Damn Phil, I'm really sorry to hear that, terrible news! Hope you get back up and running soon, no problem at all, talk in a few days!

And Phil, ever gallant, replies:

Thanks! If you see a rusty white van out driving around packed with tools, let me know :)

At O+A having your
work reviewed is
the ordeal by which
every designer
earns her stripes.

147

The Rehearsal

Pre-PARK(ing) Day jitters.
Where's the truck?
The team hits the road with grass on the floor.
Do potholes build character?

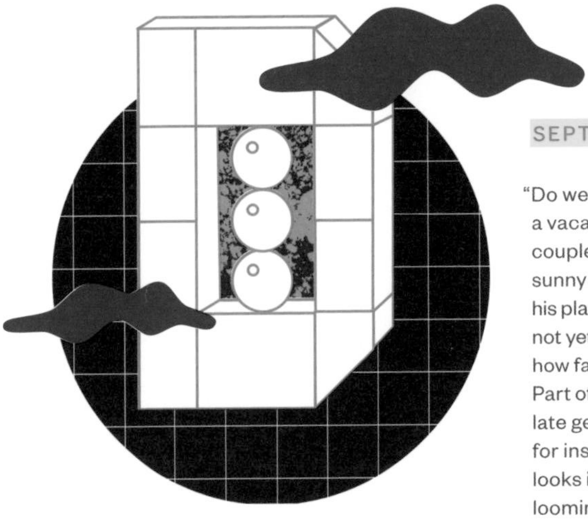

SEPTEMBER 2018

"Do we have a truck yet?" George is just back from a vacation in Italy and has been out of the loop for a couple of weeks. No doubt on the flight home from sunny Puglia he imagined returning to find much of his planning and design realized. Instead the truck is not yet back from Phil's shop. There is no clear idea of how far along Phil is, or even if the vehicle is drivable. Part of the delay, apparently, is that Doyle has been late getting the driver's and passenger's seats ready for installation. Receiving this information, George looks incredulous, like someone who sees disaster looming and knows himself to have an airtight alibi. *Hey—I was in Puglia!*

In the middle of the update, Verda clomps up the stairs. Seeing George, she stops.

"Verda, where's the truck?" George says.

He is being playful with her, but Verda flops her face into her hands. As strategist and visionary, Verda is undeniably bold, but as field commander she can fall prey to doubts. She lifts her face.

"Maybe we should call it off."

She is being playful too, but beneath all this jocular anxiety, real worry simmers—where the hell is Phil? Where is the truck? What shape will it be in? Phil's insurance covered most of the tools he lost, and by all reports he's been hard at work getting the truck ready for its kickoff project, but for the last few weeks there has been radio silence from PK Tool and Production. PARK(ing) Day starts early tomorrow morning and the truck must be transformed into what Verda calls a 'Fern Palace' (essentially a mobile pocket park) before today is done. The plants haven't arrived and because they're being donated Verda can't even call up and complain. O+A is less than 24 hours from sending a park on wheels onto the streets of San Francisco, yet at this moment there are no wheels, no park, and as it turns out, no street. Verda has learned that the organization that had agreed to host Food for Thought Truck for much of the day has, at the last minute, changed its mind. Too busy. Sorry. Maybe next year.

At least the sod is here.

- - -

On the eve of its first
real street test Food
for Thought Truck
remains an unknown
quantity. Will it
live up to the team's
expectations?

The sod?

PARK(ing) Day began in 2005 when three urban designers, John Bela, Blaine Merker and Matthew Passmore, placed a mat of real grass, a bench and a potted tree in a parking space at 1st and Mission in San Francisco, and observed how instantly and unselfconsciously passersby made use of their impromptu 'park.' After blogging about the experiment they began to get inquiries from all over the world and the idea took off in a way they had not anticipated —people from Bangkok to Nashville, Buenos Aires to Dublin—embraced PARK(ing) Day as an exercise in guerrilla urbanism and a symbolic statement in support of a greener world. Thirteen years later PARK(ing) Day is one of those global environmental observances like Earth Day or Lights Out marked on every tree-hugger's calendar. Its installations are more elaborate and more architectural than they were in year one, but a fundamental element continues to be sod.

No surprise, then, that a few weeks prior to PARK(ing) Day 2018 the focus of a Food for Thought Truck meeting is whether to clad the exterior of the truck in real or fake grass. Lauren Perich, whose idea the grass cladding is, argues for real. A new hire from New England, Lauren has arrived at O+A with a radical design sensibility that makes her instantly an ally in Verda's crusade to shake things up and an obvious recruit for Food for Thought Truck's PARK(ing) Day debut.

"They do artificial ivy," Lauren explains during a due-diligence review of potential sod suppliers—real and fake, "but within that ivy they have boxwood and agave. I estimated the whole exterior at 375 feet. They were quoting $3,800 for that."

Laughter and cross-talk rise in a swell.

"Too much!"

"Our budget is a thousand dollars!"

"What does it look like?"

"It's artificial."

"Plastic?" someone groans.

"Synthetic."

"Wouldn't that fly off the car?"

This roar of ideas and equally high-volume dissent is the way brainstorming happens at O+A, and it's why fragile creative temperaments are ill-suited to the company's sharp-elbowed design development process. Despite being new, Boston-bred Lauren holds her own in the scrum. So does Javier Gallardo,

an intern from Spain, who at the same meeting presents his idea for a supplemental attraction for PARK(ing) Day: a full-sized skeletal replica of the truck made from cardboard tubes and PVC connectors. His idea is to use the replica as a home base installation while the real truck is out and about in the city. In his soft Castilian-accented English, Javier explains to the team how he will build this 'ghost truck' four inches larger than its inspiration so the real truck can park inside it—what a great visual when the truck pulls out and the cardboard ghost is revealed...

Wait—what?

The room roars again.

– – –

Just before dark on the evening before PARK(ing) Day Phil arrives with the finished truck. Or the not-quite-finished truck. Or, okay, the nowhere-near-finished truck, but it's in good enough condition to perform its PARK(ing) Day duties. The retractable platform, last seen as an aluminum frame on the ground at Phil's Berkeley workshop, is attached to the side of the truck now. With the wood in place and the hinges and the deadbolts it looks appealingly occupational. It looks like something an itinerant blacksmith or cobbler might drive into town to set up shop. Inside? Probably just as well the design team has gone home for the day. Some of the cabinetry is installed and the upholstered bench and storage box, but there's no sink yet, no countertop, no corkboard, no glass in the windows and none of the cabinets have doors. The interior remains starkly minimal—perhaps a good thing given the dirty transformation it's about to undergo.

Verda and Primo, graphic designer Amy Young, Javier and Al come out to look at what they have to work with. Phil is eager to show off his new platform. From a fabricator's perspective this has been the trickiest part of the project—cutting the hole, building the frame, having it all fit snugly back together. Phil steps around the truck with the alacrity of a man for whom the worst is over. He unbolts the canopy window and steps inside to push it open. Two steel rods hold it in place. With the canopy up, the vehicle does indeed look like a food truck. You could serve pizza slices or tacos through that window. But it's the second part of the platform, the stage that pulls down, that Phil seems most eager to unveil. From the storage box he takes out four legs. Phil has built the platform with the capacity for eight—strong

152

enough to support a performance of *Riverdance*—but for this demonstration only the front four are needed. Each leg screws into a circular housing. It's surprisingly easy—and the connection is tight. Phil has built this stage to be idiot-proof.

But as he and Javier lower the platform, the plate securing the fourth leg to its underside dislodges from the wood. The whole thing snaps off like a stick of peppermint. Phil holds his game face—just a flicker of a frown. With all eyes on him, he is like a magician for whom the rabbit has tumbled prematurely from his sleeve.

"We may need bigger screws," he says.

Well, yes... All carpenters know the self-inflicted setback, the embarrassing glitch that would not have happened in front of the client if you had only listened to your first instinct and used the *right god-damned screws!*

While Phil sets about repairing the faulty leg, others on the team make the most of the fading light to begin transforming the truck into a park. Amy, Verda and Primo apply botanically-themed stickers to the truck's exterior—a more manageable alternative to Lauren's grass coat. Al loads up the interior of the truck with hanging ferns— delivered shortly before Phil's arrival by Habitat Horticulture. Neither operation is best performed in darkness, however, and as the only light in the parking lot comes from security lamps at the AT&T maintenance facility next door Verda makes the call to 'close the park' for the night.

Morning brings renewal and optimism. Yesterday's anxieties are swept away by sunshine, a night's sleep and the tendency of things to go smoothly on the day after a struggle. At O+A's backdoor on Howard Street, Javier finishes assembling his ghost truck, a bit smaller than he intended, not big enough to envelop the real truck, but still an impressive structure. People passing in mid-conversation fix their eyes on it and keep them there until they have walked by—is it art, a joke, a provocation? All three? Meanwhile back in the parking lot last night's metamorphosis is almost finished. The remaining vinyl stickers have been applied, more plants moved into the back and Lauren and Thomas Kany, O+A's administrative troubleshooter, are wheeling stacked rolls of sod into place for install—real sod, not synthetic. Thomas tapes down a base of plastic sheeting to keep the real dirt from overwhelming the

truck's interior. The sod unrolls like a Persian rug. In the absence of garden shears Lauren and Thomas use plain office scissors to trim each swath of Bermuda grass to fit the truck's floor plate.

It is at this point that something magical happens. Often in design one detail will pull a project into focus; one beautifully realized architectural gesture will lend weight and substance to the gestures around it. Up to now the hanging ferns and succulents-on-shelves have been prosaically what they are: plants in a truck. The unfolding of real grass on the floor gives the whole enclosure an unexpected unity—and a subversive punch. Now, the genius of Lauren's concept comes through—by including one uncanny element, the entire project is rendered uncanny. How much wilder it would have been had her original idea of cladding the exterior of the truck in real grass been realized. Of course as things worked out, it could never have happened; there wouldn't have been time and the grass almost certainly would have flown off the truck. Still, it's an affirmation of the impulse to be bold—and a good lesson for Food for Thought Truck moving forward.

When a short time later the first crew piles into the truck for its maiden voyage, there is a sense that the day is already a success. The truck really has become a park on wheels.

Although, still a park without a home. The last-minute withdrawal of the truck's principal host has blown a hole in the day's agenda. No worries. Verda likes the idea of taking the truck out fancy free, and as Javier

153

"It is at this point
that something magical
happens. Often in
design one detail will
pull a project into
focus; one beautifully
realized architectural
gesture will lend weight
and substance to the
gestures around it."

eases out of the parking lot O+A's staff gives the team a cruise-ship send-off, everyone waving and taking pictures. Javier is driving; junior staffer Aditi Saldanha rides shotgun; Lisa stands behind them as navigator; Verda and Al ride in the back.

On narrow Tehama Street, the truck moves smoothly, but as it turns onto 6th, jerky transmission and poor street maintenance turn it into a theme park ride—Green Dungeon? The hanging ferns swing from their rack like medieval flails. The canvas shoe pockets, here doubling as plant holders, threaten to disgorge their tenants with every turn. Each tap on the brakes sends potted succulents skidding on their shelves.

"Pull a right here," Lisa says, turning back to check on her passengers with a grimace.

"We're okay! We're fine!"—while the 'park' leaps and lurches.

154

The idea is to find a parking spot in Mission Bay, one of the city's vibrant new neighborhoods, home to tech HQs, medical facilities and Bayfront condos. It's not quite the neighborhood Food for Thought Truck was conceived to serve, but for a first-run rehearsal it has some advantages: it's close by; it's busy; it's an area where food trucks are common; it's a district that welcomes architectural experiment. What O+A's design visionaries haven't figured on, however, is the blunt reality of San Francisco parking. There isn't any. Not one parking space anywhere near Cisco Meraki's office or the Cal Train station. Nothing on Townsend, nothing on King. When the team spots an empty space on a passing side street, by the time they circle the block to get to it, it's gone.

Which is how Food for Thought Truck's first resting place comes to be not a design-challenged urban corner or neglected stretch of pavement as

originally envisioned, but a postcard-worthy parking spot on the Embarcadero with the Bay Bridge looming overhead: blue water, blue skies and the smell of garlic fries wafting from Red's Java House just a few steps away.

"Hey! Want a Frisbee?"

Lisa's strategy for engaging passersby is cordial ambush. Before startled pedestrians can say, "No thank you," a black saucer is sailing their way. PARK(ing) Day's team had assumed the sheer novelty of a truck hauling around a pocket park would be enough to attract attention. Pushing up the canopy, pulling down the platform, revealing the interior of real grass, they were confident their little medicine show would draw a crowd by its presence alone. But most people walking along a street are going somewhere. They are not easily diverted from their path by a Frisbee or even by a park on wheels. To the team's surprise the most effective lure turns out to be sound. At an early planning meeting Paulina had suggested bird noises to complete the park illusion. Today Javier has brought a recording of tropical warblers and speakers to broadcast it, and it is this, far more than grass on the floor, that draws people to the truck.

"We heard birds," a middle-aged woman says, walking up with a friend to peek inside, and after Lisa explains the project, says, "What a wonderful idea!"

Javier's skeleton of cardboard tubing keeps a ghost truck parked on Howard Street while the real truck drives around the city.

That Food for Thought Truck is a wonderful idea has been the consensus from Verda's first pitches to anyone who would listen. It isn't hard to get people swept up in the notion of a self-restoring road trip. Everyone who has ever dreamed of touring with a band or riding down the coast in a surfer's bus or just running away from ordinary life—which is to say pretty much everyone—can relate to this designer's version of the fantasy. Making the fantasy a reality, however, is perhaps a harder sell. After pausing to cluck over the birds and the grass, the ladies decline to step into the truck and continue on their way.

- - -

Long an enclave of poverty, drug abuse and petty crime at the center of San Francisco's commercial district, the Tenderloin is a neighborhood better suited to Food for Thought Truck's humanitarian aspirations. If any district in the city could use some remedial design assistance, this neighborhood of torn window shades and trash-strewn gutters is it. It is also conveniently situated a few blocks north of O+A's SOMA office. After a midday break back at home base, the truck goes out again, this time with Kristina Cho on board. Kristina is the first member of the truck's design team—apart from Verda—to experience the vehicle in action, and riding next to Javier up front her response to the crazy traffic and

the bumping, jerking propulsion of the truck is what Leonardo Da Vinci's might have been had he ever climbed into the helicopter he designed.

"It was terrifying!"

Once again the crisis of parking intrudes. Even in the Tenderloin, rents are rising, hip new restaurants are cropping up, boutique hotels are opening, and late on a Friday afternoon the streets are jammed with cars. Javier circles block after block, dips up urban alleyways, checks out busy downtown arteries—there is nowhere to park. As shadows lengthen and the afternoon wanes, the team's enthusiasm for the search falters. Verda is ready for a glass of wine; Kristina Da Vinci more than willing to join her, but just when everyone is about to give up... a parking place appears. From down the street Javier and Kristina spot an open space ahead —middle of the block, plenty wide enough, lots of foot traffic, a place where a park on wheels surely will be welcome. Javier guns the motor and steers the truck alongside.

Everyone groans.

On the sidewalk, smack in the middle of the space, a homeless man is passed out on his back. Lying in the sun with spittle on his lips, shirt pulled up and trousers drooping down, he is a picture of zonked-out, rock-bottom bliss. Were the park to unfold in this perfect spot its lowered platform would come to rest just inches from his nap.

Here is the challenge designers face. Reality resists improvement. The collective consciousness reflexively prefers what it already knows to someone's concept of what might be better. What design visionaries often miss is the attachment people feel to badly planned,

160

Potted plants
courtesy of Habitat
Horticulture turn the
truck's interior into
Verda's Fern Palace.

but familiar surroundings. In the context of design, familiarity often breeds not contempt, but contentment. Some architectural thinking takes it beyond familiarity. Rem Koolhaas has made a case for the psychological attraction of not-so-nice environments. "In every life," he told *Strelka* magazine, "there needs to be maybe a cocktail of anxiety, disbelief, insecurity, and creativity. I think that those areas are actually quite close together and I think that to be too certain of your environment and to have an environment that is only affirming a secure situation is probably not a big blessing in the end." It's an idea that echoes Verda's theories about friction in the workplace. After a quarter-century of shaping offices to be comfortable and easy to use, she has come to question the long-term impact of all this ease. Is it making us weaker? Less capable? Less able to solve problems? For most of civilization adversity has been an acknowledged builder of character. Do we really want to design adversity out of existence? To say nothing of the pleasure people take in their not-so-nice surroundings. It's not hard to guess what two words this homeless man passed out on the sidewalk would say if O+A woke him to a chorus of birdsong and invited him into a green park on wheels.

Probably not "Thank you."

161

The Road: South & East Bay

Shark alert!
Nikki and Kayla build a prototype.
Lucha libre under the stars.
Deliverance through mini-golf.

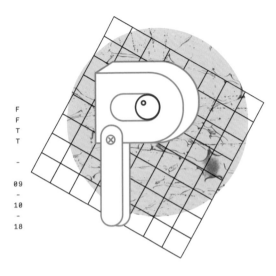

F
F
T
T

-

09

-

10

-

18

166

SEPTEMBER-OCTOBER 2018

PARK(ing) Day proves to be a good dress rehearsal for driving the truck and anticipating operational kinks—the platform legs, for example, are too long for the high curbs along the Embarcadero. The stage when it came down sloped backwards on the waterfront. (Note to Phil: please provide a second set of shorter legs for extra-high curbs.) A good trial run, then, for the truck as a piece of machinery, but it remains to be seen how useful this rehearsal will be for design. PARK(ing) Day, after all, is a more ethereal exercise than the others under consideration. It's a one-day pop-up, a fantasy project, more performance art than practical build. A better test of Food for Thought Truck's program will be the upcoming partnership with Public Space Authority on projects in the South and East Bay.

It was Rachelle Meneses, Food for Thought Truck's kickoff project manager, who put the team in touch with Marie Millares from Public Space Authority. Rachelle got pulled off the truck team early when her management skills were more urgently needed on O+A jobs that paid, but Verda and Marie quickly connected and saw the synchronicity of their two initiatives. Public Space Authority is a nonprofit dedicated to reviving underused public spaces through architectural, entrepreneurial and artistic interventions—precisely the sort of thing Food for Thought Truck has in mind for itself.

In their first meeting at O+A's office Marie laid out a series of projects, any one of which would be ideal for the truck's first effort outside of San Francisco. PSA was partnering with the San Jose Flea Market to upgrade merchant stalls and attract a younger crowd. It was working with the MOMENT Organization to assist pop-up retailers in San Jose's San Pedro Square. In the East Bay city of Fremont it was developing a vacant lot left behind by a defunct shopping center. From Food for Thought Truck's perspective each of these projects had the right scale of need, the right grassroots provenance and the right specificity of purpose for the truck team's goals and expertise. In short, a perfect fit.

FFTT
-
09
-
10
-
18

167

Sometimes community
improvement arrives
disguised as something
else. In Fremont
it's lucha libre.

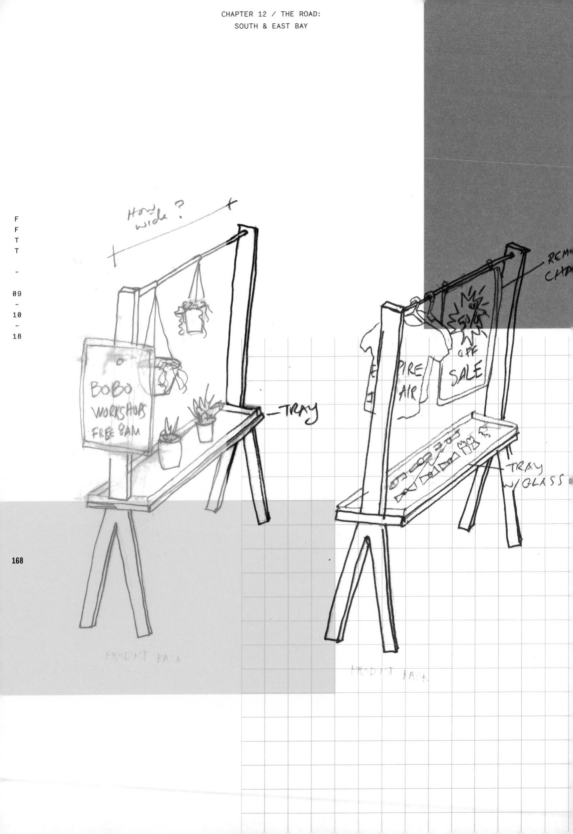

The team's first preference was, predictably, the Flea Market. Who wouldn't want to hang out at a giant open market that's been in operation for over half a century? Food for Thought Truck held an early design charrette to brainstorm attractions that would draw a younger demographic (all-night raves, tattoo parlors, outdoor movies, dog grooming, etc.) and drew up some preliminary sketches for stall design that would give the market an architectural makeover—but in the end the calendar killed the project. The Flea Market's and the truck's operating schedules could not align.

For its first real project, then, Food for Thought Truck turned to San Pedro Square.

- - -

With a population of 1.035 million San Jose is the largest city in the Bay Area. The capital of Silicon Valley, the area's most Hispanic city, the city with the warmest, driest climate—it has a lot going for it, and yet on an ordinary weekday San Jose can feel strangely vacant. Its wide streets and bare storefronts surrounded by office towers do not convey the wealth that is concentrated here. Unlike San Francisco or Oakland or Berkeley, San Jose lacks the density to create a truly urban texture. This part of California has had an impact on the rest of the world to rival that of Hollywood—but where is everybody?

Early one morning in October, Verda meets Marie and Kevin Biggers of San Jose Made outside the MOMENT shops in San Pedro Square. San Pedro is the oldest part of the city, site of an adobe landmark dating back to the 18th century and home to a stretch of popular restaurants and nightspots that make it a San Jose destination. Every Friday from May to November its main street closes to traffic to make way for a farmers' market. In the parking garage near the end of the street, MOMENT has contracted with four small-business owners to open pop-up shops. Food for Thought Truck proposes to help these pop-ups with store design, signage—whatever they need!

"What are the permit requirements for hanging banners from those things?" Verda asks, pointing to a tall street lamp from which a big MOMENT banner designed by Food for Thought Truck would wave most handsomely.

Marie looks doubtful. "I don't know if it's a permit. I think it's more about who owns it. The Sharks own those."

Kevin adds, "Even though it's a city parking structure it's owned by The Sharks. Any substantial changes

Unlike San Francisco or Oakland or Berkeley, San Jose lacks the density to create a truly urban texture. This part of California has had an impact on the rest of the world to rival that of Hollywood—but where is everybody?

F
F
T
T
-
09
-
10
-
18

to this structure kind of have to be approved by The Sharks."

"And is it usually something Sharks-related that's mounted there?" Verda asks.

Marie says, "Almost always."

The Sharks. A criminal network with its teeth in every profit-making enterprise in the city? A cadre of Silicon Valley billionaires who rule San Jose like their personal duchy? No, actually it's an ice hockey team in a city where ice rarely forms. Somehow this winter sport franchise has become the beating heart of sunny San Jose—and apparently a major property owner in the city.

Nix the banners, then. Nix, too, any plans for a pocket park in front of the MOMENT shops, a spin-off idea from PARK(ing) Day. A pocket park already exists— and it's a nice one, extending the full length of the storefronts. Not a lot to be added there. Not a lot to be added in the stores either. Retail design had seemed a fun prospect, especially if it would help a young merchant get her shop off the ground—but Sarah Lim of Fractal Flora and Angie Chua of Bobo Design (the other two shops are closed for the day) have already set up distinctive boutiques. They're cozy; they're inviting; they have personality. What they lack is basic infrastructure: running water, storage space, protection from the elements. These young shopkeepers need plumbers and structural engineers—not interior design missionaries.

Interior designers appreciate buildings with 'good bones.' They execute projects in such buildings with the same respect that musicians bring to a concert hall with notably fine acoustics. Some interior designers appreciate, also, 'terrible bones'—i.e. buildings with serious architectural shortcomings, oddly

169

The Sharks. A criminal
network with its teeth
in every profit-making
enterprise in the city?
A cadre of Silicon
Valley billionaires who
rule San Jose like their
personal duchy?

F
F
T
T

-

09
-
10
-
18

shaped spaces, poor circulation. Transforming such
a space into an appealing and useful interior is the
sort of challenge many in the profession relish.
What no one in the profession relishes is working
where the design is more or less done. Designers do
not flourish in another bird's nest, and these MOMENT
retailers have set up their nests most ably.

- - -

Even so, a few weeks after Verda's site visit and subse-
quent communications with Sarah and Angie, Chase
drives the Food for Thought Truck down to San Jose
to open it up at the Friday farmers' market. Early in
the morning as the usual vendors set up their stalls for
locally grown fruits and vegetables, locally harvested
nuts, fresh flowers, home-made honey and cheese, the
team unpacks in front of the MOMENT shops its own
harvest of design.

Nikki Hall and Kayla Goldberg (a recent recruit to
the truck's San Jose team) have been working with
Javier Gallardo—he of the PARK(ing) Day cardboard-
tube ghost truck—to design another cardboard
structure. Of all the design needs mentioned by the
shopkeepers the one that seemed most addressable
by Food for Thought Truck was signage and display.
Nikki, Kayla and Verda now assemble a cardboard
model that combines both needs in a hybrid unit—
bottom half serving as base and chalkboard, top half
pairing shelves with a rack for hanging merchan-
dise. It's the sort of multi-task design that O+A favors
—simple, attractive, elegantly functional, adapt-
able to many uses. If they get a green light today
the team will build a few of these units out of wood
and give them to the shops free of charge. It comes
as something of a surprise then, that none of the
MOMENT retailers seem particularly enthusiastic.
Yeah, they're nice; not sure where we'd put them...
It is not a response to inspire an eager return to the
drawing board.

Meanwhile some quirky stools specially designed
for and donated to Food for Thought Truck by one
of O+A's long-time furniture partners get a first
try-out and that, too, becomes a wobbly debut.
Literally wobbly. The rounded base of the stool
which accounts for its distinctive look makes it an
unsteady seat. You must place your legs just so or
risk tumbling off. Assessing the liability issues, the
team pulls the stools off the sidewalk minutes after
putting them out.

With the prototype a yawn and the hip new stools
a swift trip to the ground on your butt, Food for
Thought Truck's morning at the farmers' market
devolves into a replay of its morning on the
Embarcadero, minus the grass and bird sounds:
"Want a Frisbee?"

A visiting team of journalists from Tokyo are on
hand to record the day for an upcoming, all-O+A issue
of *Worksight* magazine. They interview Verda and
take pictures of Nikki and Kayla building the display
unit. Fortunately their English isn't good enough to
pick up on the day's odd vibe. People passing through
the farmers' market don't seem to get what the truck
is about. Is somebody running for office? Is somebody
selling a phone/data plan? For the team you could call
it 'a learning moment,' this realization at San Pedro
Square, that after months of planning, programming
and visualization, Food for Thought Truck's purpose
still isn't clear.

A young couple approaches pushing an empty
stroller while their toddler clops one foot in front of
the other alongside.
"Care for a Frisbee?" Al asks, leaning in.
Dad squints one eye. "How much?"

- - -

Food for Thought Truck's Fremont project gets
off to a better start.

In 2017 bulldozers took down the terracotta-roofed
buildings of Town Fair Shopping Center, a 40-year-
old, 22,000-square-foot commercial development
that had grown too dated for its prime city-center
location. Town Fair was not a deluxe retail mall with
a big anchor tenant like Macy's or Nordstrom's. It was
a modest shopping center of old-fashioned open-air
design that had by the time of its demise very little
actual 'shopping' left. Its major tenants were small
businesses like China Chili Restaurant, Entourage
Beauty Salon, BJ Travel Service and a Genius Kids
tutoring franchise. Demolition cleared the way for

170

a major civic center development by the City of Fremont, but rather than let the vacant lot lie idle for the years it would take to get that project up and running, the city and its partners chose Public Space Authority to create a temporary community plaza on the site.

The spirit of PSA's development is robustly on view one Thursday evening when Verda, Lisa and Al bring the truck to Fremont for a Town Fair Plaza pro-wrestling match. Under the old shopping center sign that is all that remains of the former Town Fair, a Buckminster Fuller-style geodesic dome forms the canopy that shelters the evening's revelries. The dome is Town Fair Plaza's most striking feature. Festooned with lights, it looks like a planetary settler's camp in a sci-fi epic. Surely the characters howling and throwing body slams in the ring could be sci-fi creatures? A steam-punk dude in top-hatted Victoriana, a little dude decked out in lucha libre glory, a big bearded dude in black T-shirt and shredded jeans. Despite the significant size differential Little Lucha Libre seems to be mopping the floor with Big Bearded Dude. Meanwhile the audience of families with young children keep up a barrage of catcalls and taunts, received with outsized umbrage by the villains in the ring.

This is interactive community circus, and while it's amped up to an absurdist pitch, it's a pretty good example of what Public Space Authority likes to do—take an unpromising public site, use design to make it more inviting (that dome, those lights), enlist the community to apply their talents to turn it into something transcendent (a battle of the titans every Thursday night). You never know what inspiration a situation like that might spark.

In the hubbub of heckling and faux backtalk, the blowing horns and derisive clapping, a child's voice rings out with the clarity of a California sunset, a jeer at the beefy combatants that wins the night for creativity:

"Eat some salad!" the kid yells.

– – –

It is quieter at Town Fair Plaza on the afternoon Food for Thought Truck hosts a design charrette. When the plaza is not employed as a pro-wrestling venue, it's a sunny, open space for parents to bring their kids. It's a destination for food trucks (real ones) and a place where the maker community gathers for fairs and expositions. There's a tetherball court, a picnic area, a beer garden and a mini-golf course. Actually 'course' is too grand a word for the three novelty golf holes currently in operation

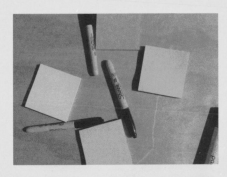

The sketch the team selects for further development is an Olympic ice rink with gold medalist and Fremont native Kristi Yamaguchi a spinning obstacle in the center. If you hit the ball too hard, it gutters like a bowling ball and rolls back to the tee to taunt you.

F
F
T
T
-
09
-
10
-
18

—and that is the subject of Food for Thought Truck's charrette.

On a bright, breezy day the team pins questions to the side of the truck and invites a small group of local participants to write answers on Post It notes to questions like: What are Fremont's loveliest landmarks? What are its ugliest? What do you love most about living in Fremont? Describe Fremont in one word or two. ("Dumplings!" one enthusiast writes.) With these themes to guide them the group assembles at a community art table and draws up their ideas for a fourth Fremont-themed mini-golf attraction. Someone suggests a green with a giant wild goose looming over it (in recognition of that bird's omnipresence in Fremont). Someone imagines a twisting motorway, someone else an auto assembly line (Fremont is the Bay Area's car manufacturing center.) Someone draws a dragon—you hit the ball in its mouth and it comes out the tail.

The sketch the team selects for further development is an Olympic ice rink with gold medalist and Fremont native Kristi Yamaguchi a spinning obstacle in the center. If you hit the ball too hard, it gutters like a bowling ball and rolls back to the tee to taunt you. It's a fairly complicated structure with engineering elements and some artful flourishes—and though Javier works out the basic construction drawings, for once he does not have to build it himself. Verda meets with a carpenter a week later at Town Fair.

"These are all nominal, right?" the carpenter asks looking at the construction drawings. "You don't have a plus or minus one thousandth of an inch tolerance required?" He laughs. "That's why I like

174

working with wood. I've worked with metal most of my life and it's always, 'Hell, dude. It can't almost be right. It has to be exactly right.'"

"For mini-golf it doesn't have to be too precise," Verda says. "We're not looking for perfection."

But even 'short of perfection' proves too high a bar.

Before the golf feature can be quite finished; before the putting green is nailed down and the vinyl 'ice-traps' secured; the wooden figures cut out and painted and the whole structure assembled and connected to the existing course; before anyone can see what Food for Thought Truck has been working on in Fremont, the carpenter for whom 'almost right' is right enough, flies home to Abu Dhabi for a month-long family visit. Abruptly the project has to be shelved.

(Later, Verda will return to it with another carpenter recruited from Bakersfield, and they will nail the thing together. She, and O+A designer Emily Cano will paint the wooden figures: the ice skater and the Olympic judges. Verda will spend hours painting individual faces on the crowd of wooden onlookers. The Kristi Yamaguchi golf feature will debut at Town Fair Plaza's 'Weird Science Fair' on December 15, 2018 and will prove immensely popular, especially with young children. Later it will be a Food for Thought Truck project everyone can feel good about. But at this moment, coming after San Jose's inconclusive results, the sudden shelving of Fremont hits the team like a wave of nausea.)

On the eve of Food for Thought Truck's week-long trip to Bakersfield, the largest commitment of money and resources since O+A purchased the truck, the underwhelming outcomes in San Jose and Fremont leave some at O+A questioning the whole project. "Is the truck a fizzle?" one staff member who is not on the team asks confidentially another who is. Throughout the office the sense of an experiment going awry simmers beneath the upbeat talk. Whenever Food for Thought Truck is mentioned at weekly staff meetings—which is often—the happy buzzwords do not waver: creative road trip, guerilla design, thinking out of the box; but as those words are spoken some at O+A working long hours on big corporate projects may be excused for thinking other words:

Mini-golf?

For Food for Thought Truck, Bakersfield is make or break.

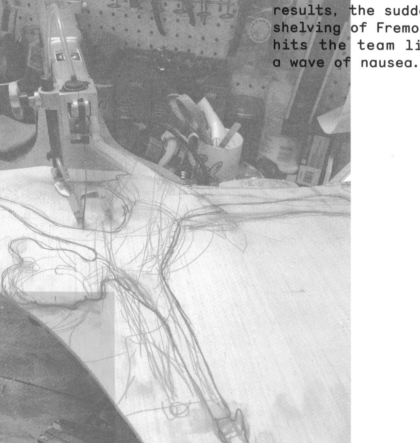

The Kristi Yamaguchi golf feature will debut at Town Fair Plaza's Weird Science Fair on December 15, 2018 and will prove immensely popular, especially with young children. Later it will be a Food for Thought Truck project everyone can feel good about. But at this moment coming after San Jose's inconclusive results, the sudden shelving of Fremont hits the team like a wave of nausea.

F
F
T
T

-

09
-
10
-
18

177

179

The Road:
Bakersfield I

A legendary architect's last stand.
Eastchester steps up.
At last: cruising speed.
Ariel steals the show.

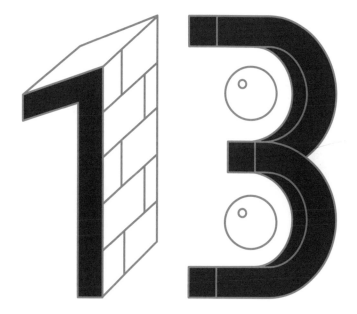

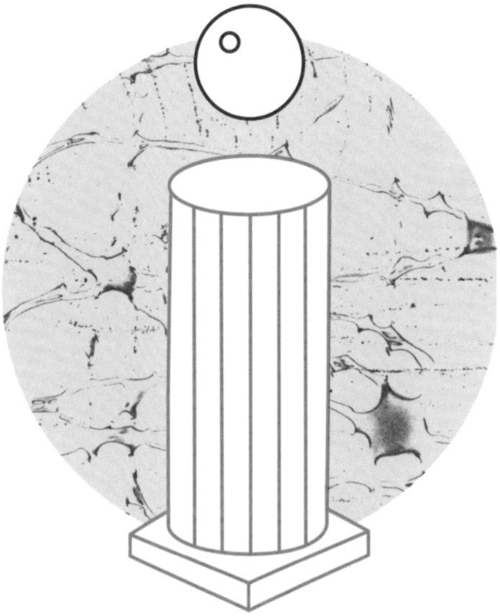

NOVEMBER 2018

In the summer of 1958 Mildred Ablin, a registered nurse and wife of a Bakersfield neurosurgeon, Dr. George Ablin, wrote a letter to Frank Lloyd Wright:

Dear Mr Wright:

As former students and residents from the University of Madison Wisconsin and having always been thrilled by your work of which there is no representation here in Bakersfield, we were wondering if it is possible for you and practical for us to have you design a home for us and our young family of six and probably seven children...

As an example of cramming everything you want to say into one sentence before the great man can throw your letter away, this was not only a shrewdly constructed opener; it also provided a charming sample of the understated pride that is a notable characteristic of people from Bakersfield. After describing the site on which she and her husband wished to build, Mrs Ablin ended by noting, "Our means are modest; those of a young surgeon," and went on to ask Wright for a referral to another architect if he was not interested.

The Ablin House became one of Frank Lloyd Wright's last projects. He designed it in 1958 and died the next year. Construction was finished in 1961. Situated on a hilltop amidst grapefruit and pomegranate trees, the house is a structural conjugation of triangles—a large triangular window looking out to the Sierra Nevada mountains, triangular patterns in the finishes and furniture, a triangular swimming pool. It has a showcase living room and a welcoming kitchen and enough bedrooms to accommodate the Ablins' big family—which it did for many years.

Today the house is home only to visitors. It is maintained and administered as a Bakersfield cultural landmark by architectural historian David Coffey. David is possibly the foremost authority on Bakersfield's built environment. He lives in a Richard Neutra house and can regale you with stories about the provenance and particulars of notable buildings all over town.

Bakersfield evokes
a California that
once lured coastal
transplants in
droves—sunshine,
orange trees,
the open road.

He offers use of the Ablin House free of charge to visiting artists and architects, and when he learned of Food for Thought Truck's visit from Daniel Cater graciously suggested the team stay there.

Which is how Alex Pokas and Lauren Harrison come to be inching up the driveway on Friday evening with no light to guide them but the truck's high beams. "When I was younger," Lauren says, "my dad told me one of the best pieces of advice he ever got was: Don't arrive in the dark." But Lauren and Alex have pulled into Bakersfield well after sundown—Alex driving, Lauren navigating—the conclusion of a long day on the road from San Francisco. As new-ish designers at O+A both Alex and Lauren bring to this expedition the enthusiasm for new experience that new hires often exhibit (must exhibit) for whatever is thrown at them. Loose steering wheel? Long trek down I-5? Smelly agricultural miles? It's all part of the 'fun.' Still, the dark neighborhood, the hidden house, the uncertain reception from a town they don't know... it all adds up to a particular kind of fatigue. Easing up this steep driveway to they know not what, Food for Thought Truck's ambassadors admit to some anxiety.

"I thought it was a little creepy," Lauren says.

- - -

Al McKee and Daniel Cater are waiting at the house, Al having arrived earlier by train. After a welcome-to-Bakersfield glass of wine, Daniel takes everyone on a night tour of Downtown, a quick preview of the hospitable local culture already suggested by David Coffey's generosity. At Café Smitten, at a Tiki bar, at a Caribbean restaurant, friends call out to Daniel. The whole town seems to know him. Bakersfield is not small statistically. As of 2018, its population is approaching 400,000, and yet on this night there is a Frank Capra quality to the shouts hello across noisy rooms. Daniel moves through these encounters with the lanky good humor of a young Jimmy Stewart.

Back at the house at evening's end, Lauren, Alex and Al tour the bedrooms to decide who will sleep where. After the long travel day and dinner festivities everyone is beat. You might think sleep would come without a hitch, but something about the house remains unsettling; the cavernous spaces, the old man's presence.

Verda arrives a little before 1:00am. Earlier in the evening she flew from Chicago to Los Angeles and hired an Uber car to drive her to Bakersfield—a

two-hour journey, "listening to Persian music all the way." Now her Iranian driver gives her a hug in the driveway of Ablin House, and Al comes out to greet her. Verda is tired and ready for bed.

"Don't mind the ghosts," Al says

For the rest of the week in Bakersfield the Frank Lloyd Wright house doubles as historic architectural opportunity of a lifetime—thank you, David Coffey; and macabre running joke for the ghoulishly-inclined —thank you, Frank Lloyd Wright. Lauren finds a faint child's footprint in the waxed surface of the master bedroom floor. Al claims to hear a little girl singing behind the closed door of a music room. Turkey vultures perch in the treetops outside. When Paulina drives in from the Bay Area on Saturday she contributes a story from Wright's gruesome past: a crazed servant, an ax murder, death by starvation. "This is Wikipedia!" she cries. "I'm not making this up!" Still, after a couple of days everyone relaxes.

"I do love the house," Paulina says during lunch at Café Smitten on Sunday.

"I feel like the two coolest things so far," Alex says, "are using the kitchen and taking a shower." She means access to a Frank Lloyd Wright house is usually a look-but-don't-touch tour. It's kind of a trip actually to live in one. But Lauren can't resist:

"When you first came out of the bathroom that night saying the shower was a little freaky? Well, supposedly Frank Lloyd Wright was a womanizer, and I was thinking maybe it's his ghost watching you in the shower."

Everyone shivers. Everyone laughs.

- - -

On Saturday morning Verda, Alex, Lauren and Al—Paulina has yet to arrive at this point—take the Food for Thought Truck to its designated place in the parking lot outside Café Smitten. In advance of the trip to Bakersfield the design team had done a Google Earth search of this spot, which Daniel had assured them was a lively hub of the downtown area—plenty of foot traffic, a welcoming vibe, nice folks. On Google Earth the café looked welcoming enough, but the neighborhood around it seemed eerily depopulated—a flat, bleak landscape with scarcely a soul in sight. You wouldn't call it an urban landscape because it looked like something out of *The Last Picture Show*. Clicking on the Google Earth arrow and traveling up 18th Street past an auto body shop and a Chinese restaurant, past parking lots and intersections strangely bereft of cars, some Food for Thought Truckers experienced a sinking feeling. Was this another disappointment in the works? After all the planning and anticipation, would Bakersfield be a replay of San Jose?

Now sunlight and reality expose the limitations of Google Earth. For one thing the block is hardly depopulated. On a Saturday morning Café Smitten is buzzing. The people sitting outside and looking up from their breakfasts as the truck pulls in span a demographic spectrum from retired married couples settled in Bakersfield for its affordability and warm weather (which the team expected) to tattooed young adventurers—well, they look like adventurers—who would not be out of place in the basecamp for an assault on Everest (which the team had not envisioned). Bikers, skateboarders, laptop lingerers, lovers holding hands, kids holding cell phones—really, this crowd lining up for mushroom omelettes, quinoa bowls and state-of-the-art lattes does not, at first glance, communicate 'small town' to the visiting San Franciscans. Café Smitten could be a hangout in the Mission or on New York's Lower East Side. But if the surface finish feels urban, the undercoat suggests something closer to a village.

Those bikers, for example. A group of motor-cyclists in black leather and bandanas are gathered in the parking lot next to their bikes. Back in San Francisco or Oakland you would step around any impromptu assembly of leather-clad bikers in a parking lot, but as the Food for Thought Truckers climb down from their vehicle, one of the bad dudes pulls off his helmet. "David!" It's David Coffey, the historian and caretaker of Ablin House. That pattern of surprise—I think I know what I'm looking at; oh wait, maybe I don't—repeats itself throughout the day, and each time it reveals a facet of Bakersfield that is deeper and more nuanced than the 'sophi-sticates' from San Francisco first assume.

As they're lifting the canopy and pulling down the platform to set up the truck, the team can feel eyes on them from the direction of the café. Back in San Francisco Alex, Lauren and Kristina devised a series of activities for the week. There's a mapping exercise scheduled for today and a Pecha Kucha presentation to wrap up the evening (20 slides, 20 seconds of commentary for each). Of course one of the fundamentals of design is that place redraws plans. Will these ideas, that seemed promising at

an O+A worktable in San Francisco, pan out with real people in Bakersfield? Will anyone care? As soon as the truck is open, the Frisbees and stickers and postcards laid out, the posters erected, the maps and markers assembled, one of the retirees gets up from his breakfast table and saunters over.

"Is this the truck from San Francisco?" he says.

Daniel Cater has done his advance work well.

- - -

"Imagine Eastchester" is the title of this Food for Thought Truck project. It is also the purpose of the exercise. For a city of its size Bakersfield has an un-usually sharp neighborhood awareness—Downtown, Westchester, Seven Oaks, East Bakersfield all have distinct geographical and cultural identities, almost tribal identities. Eastchester is a part of Downtown that is emerging after a period of underdevelopment, and there's a sense that the year ahead is crucial— or could be. One of Daniel's stated goals for Food for Thought Truck's visit is that it demonstrate that Bakersfield really is changing, that people outside are interested and that Eastchester could be everything its advocates want it to be. "Are the things we're doing really impactful," he says, "or are we just so involved

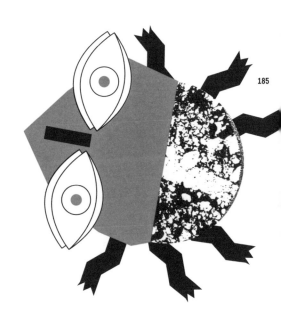

F
F
T
T

-

11
-
18

For the rest of the week
in Bakersfield the Frank
Lloyd Wright house doubles
as historic architectural
opportunity of a lifetime—
thank you, David Coffey;
and macabre running joke
for the ghoulishly-
inclined—thank you, Frank
Lloyd Wright.

186

F
F
T
T
-
11
-
18

ꜰ ꜰ ꜰ with them that we think they're having an impact?"
Food for Thought Truck is in town for a week primarily
188 to facilitate conversation and to be outside agitators
for initiatives already in motion.

In that respect the mapping exercise is a perfect
conversation starter. Alex and Lauren have printed a
stack of one-page street maps of the downtown area
and everyone who steps up to chat is urged to "draw
what you think are the boundaries of Eastchester."
One woman dashes a tight circle around Café
Smitten: "That's pretty much it." But most people
take a more expansive view. Eastchester in the minds
of its residents proves an urban amoeba, its shape
and scope varying with the cartographer. Some folks
draw a rectangle roughly in the center of downtown,
some a box that takes in everything east of Chester
Street, but many gerrymander a border around their
favorite nightspots, parks and stores. Almost everyone
loves the idea of tailoring a neighborhood to his or
her personal specifications.

Alex talks to a guy who not only draws the borders
of Eastchester, but starts filling in things he'd like to
see there. He is jumping the gun a bit—this is an activity
planned for later in the week—but his excitement is
infectious. "This is where I want to see a beer garden,"
he tells her, marking the spot. "This would be so cool.
I really hope this happens."

Verda talks to two ladies who collaborate on their
map, making sure it includes where they live. Peeking at
someone else's boundaries, one says to the other, "They
left us out." It seems a good sign that people want to be
residents of Eastchester.

Lauren talks at length with another shop owner on
18th Street. "This guy has been here for 30 years,"
she says, "kind of holding down the fort without
a whole lot going on. He's so thrilled that change
is coming. In San Francisco people get bitter
about all the changes that are happening. It's
refreshing to meet a local person who's appreciative
of change."

Which is not to say everyone in Bakersfield imagines Eastchester the same way. A silver-haired man steps up to the truck's display, wrinkling his nose at the maps, the hopeful messages, the bright colors. His wife wears the fixed smile of someone who knows what's coming: "Well, they need to clean it up," the man says to Verda. "I'm not crazy about all the porn shops and pawn shops. They need to clean all that out if they want a nice neighborhood here, because right now it's not a nice neighborhood. I'm just telling you the truth, okay? It's not a place you'd want to bring your family. I don't come over here unless I have my gun with me or my knife." Verda continues to look him in the eye, but other staffers in earshot give his person a discreet once-over to see if any weaponry is evident. (He's clean, as the cops say after a frisk.) "And this part of town," the man continues, pointing to a map. "I wouldn't go there unless a black person took me. I wouldn't even go there."

His wife's smile travels farther and farther away from the moment.

"Thanks for your feedback," Verda says.

Really, though, this is a minority view. The overwhelming consensus, as expressed by people who actually live or do business (unarmed) in the community, is that Eastchester truly is on the verge of something. The mood of the place—to the extent it is readable by first-time visitors on a bright fall Saturday in the parking lot of Café Smitten—is one of hope, enthusiasm and confidence in the change that is coming.

"It's really crazy how… what's it called when you're for your team?" Verda says.

"Team spirit?"

"Team spirit. How strong the team spirit is here."

"And everybody's so nice," Lauren adds.

A young man walks out of Café Smitten. He's a big guy with a big beard and his hair tied up in a bun on his head. His T-shirt references some music festival. He has just had lunch or a coffee and is heading out into his Saturday afternoon. As he passes his eyes land on the image boards the team have set up on easels outside the truck. "Have you heard about our project?" Al asks. In San Francisco or San Jose this guy would keep going, smile perhaps or lift an apologetic hand, but keep walking. Here in Bakersfield, he stops.

"Tell me about it," he says.

- - -

Almost everyone is approachable in the early afternoon, and quite a few of the locals who stop at the truck promise to come back for the Pecha Kucha at the end of the day. Even so, as the sun dips, it comes as a surprise to the Food for Thought Truck folks that people who dropped by earlier do in fact return. To see people filling up the seats at Café Smitten's outdoor tables, perching on its hay bales and standing around the truck waiting for the show to begin gives this first day wrap-up one last surge of energy. Even the setup for the Pecha Kucha becomes an exercise in community engagement. Paulina has brought her projector and screen from Oakland, and Café Smitten has volunteered a microphone, extension cord and power outlet, but at the last minute the team discovers they don't have the right cable to connect the laptop to the projector. Pecha Kucha without pictures is just a series of speeches, and for a few moments it looks like the day will end in snores. Then a friend of Daniel's steps up. "What kind of cord do you need?" He sprints across the parking lot to his apartment in the townhomes and comes back with the show-saving connector.

"Thank you all for coming…" Verda begins.

Verda's Pecha Kucha is an introduction to O+A and the Food for Thought Truck project, and as leader of the team she allows herself more than 20 slides and more than 20 seconds each to speak about them. Noblesse oblige. Verda's casual approach to the rules of Pecha Kucha takes pressure off the other presenters. Austin Smith, a Bakersfield realtor and planner; Scott Hellman, a local developer; Al McKee from O+A and Daniel Cater all speak on some variation of how Eastchester can change, what Eastchester might become. But the evening belongs to Ariel Dyer, a Bakersfield musician and librarian. Speaking from notes on file cards, Ariel leans into the microphone and right into the spirit of the day:

"In order for a community to thrive, we should be celebrating two types of people: the people who show up and the people dedicated to putting themselves out there consistently whether anyone shows up or not."

With that declaration Ariel pulls together everyone in the plaza, the local folks who have shown up all afternoon and the designers from San Francisco who have traveled all this way to meet them. "I'm a local musician," she continues. "I play often at Café Smitten and am grateful for the opportunity. I play my heart out to a full house, and I still give every ounce of effort

F
F
T
T

-

11

-

18

190

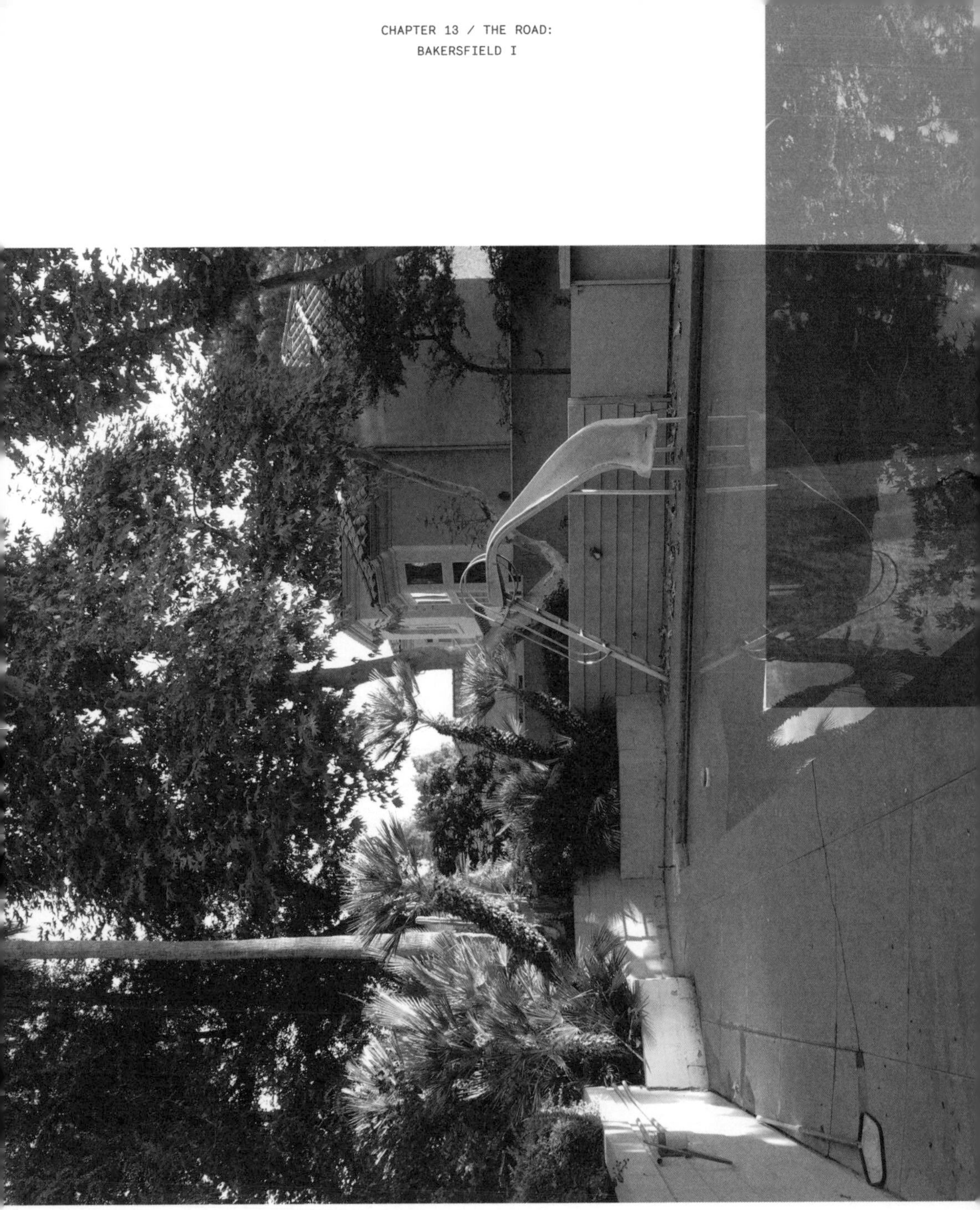

The triangular
pool at Ablin House
reprises in blue
water the geometry
the house preserves
in brick and stone.

"The trick is to plant
your feet and play to
your audience, even if
it's an audience of one."

if I'm singing to one person or to none. I play whether the people show up or not. I think the group that is building up Eastchester is full of people like that."

Right at the top of her presentation, not even 20 seconds in, Ariel has articulated the day's discovery, maybe even Food for Thought Truck's discovery: that all-out effort is outcome enough and achievement is a flower that blossoms on that stem.

As she speaks, a feeling comes over the Food for Thought Truck team. It's the feeling that hit when Chase and Marbel first drove the truck onto O+A's parking lot in January and that hit again on PARK(ing) Day in San Francisco months later when the sod was laid and the truck suddenly turned into a park. It's the feeling the visiting design students experienced during Design Week's Studio Crawl

when the truck was nothing but an empty vessel into which they could pour their aspirations and that the design team experienced a short time later when the fully-dressed truck unpacked for the first time at the Farmers' Market in San Pedro Square. It's a feeling of possibility, the realization that things do sometimes work out.

After all the anxieties attendant on this project —would anyone come? would the work be worthy?— Day One in Bakersfield has more than lived up to expectations. The energy pulsing through Eastchester and the generosity of its citizens in embracing a band of outsiders looking critically at their city is the best demonstration yet of Food for Thought Truck's concept. And now, leaning into the microphone, this young woman from Bakersfield gives voice to that energy and generosity. Describing programs she has created at the library, she underscores the importance of persistence—imagination, yes; creativity, yes; boldness of spirit, by all means; but driving it all: persistence.

"I still plan some programs that few people show up to," Ariel concludes. "I still play some shows to mostly empty rooms. Those things still happen, though less often than when I started." She looks up from her note card. The assembled dreamers of Eastchester and their guests are beaming. "The trick is to plant your feet and play to your audience, even if it's an audience of one."

194

FFTT
-
11
-
18

195

F
F
T
T

-

11
-
18

196

198

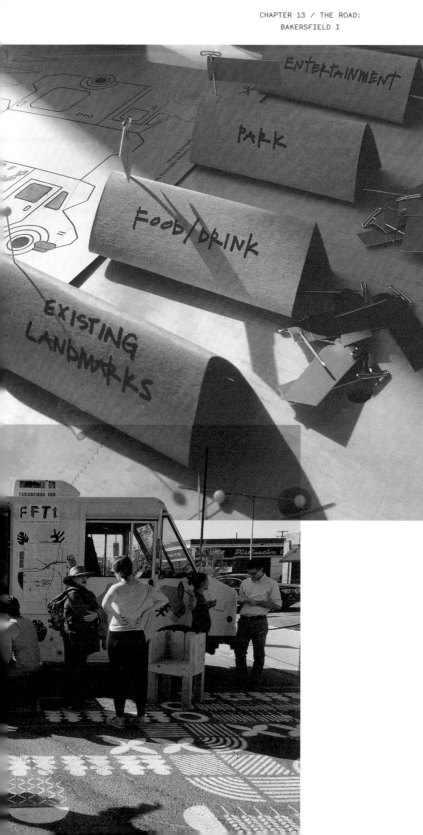

ENTERTAINMENT

PARK

FOOD/DRINK

EXISTING
LANDMARKS

FFTT - 11 - 18

FFT1
FOOD FOR THOUGHT TRUCK

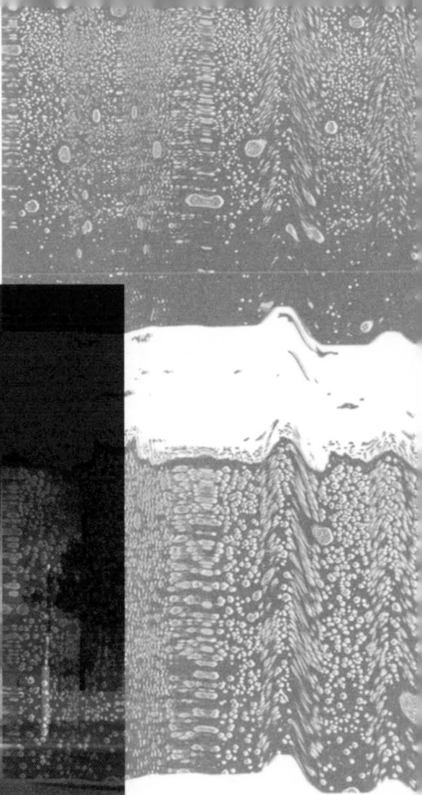

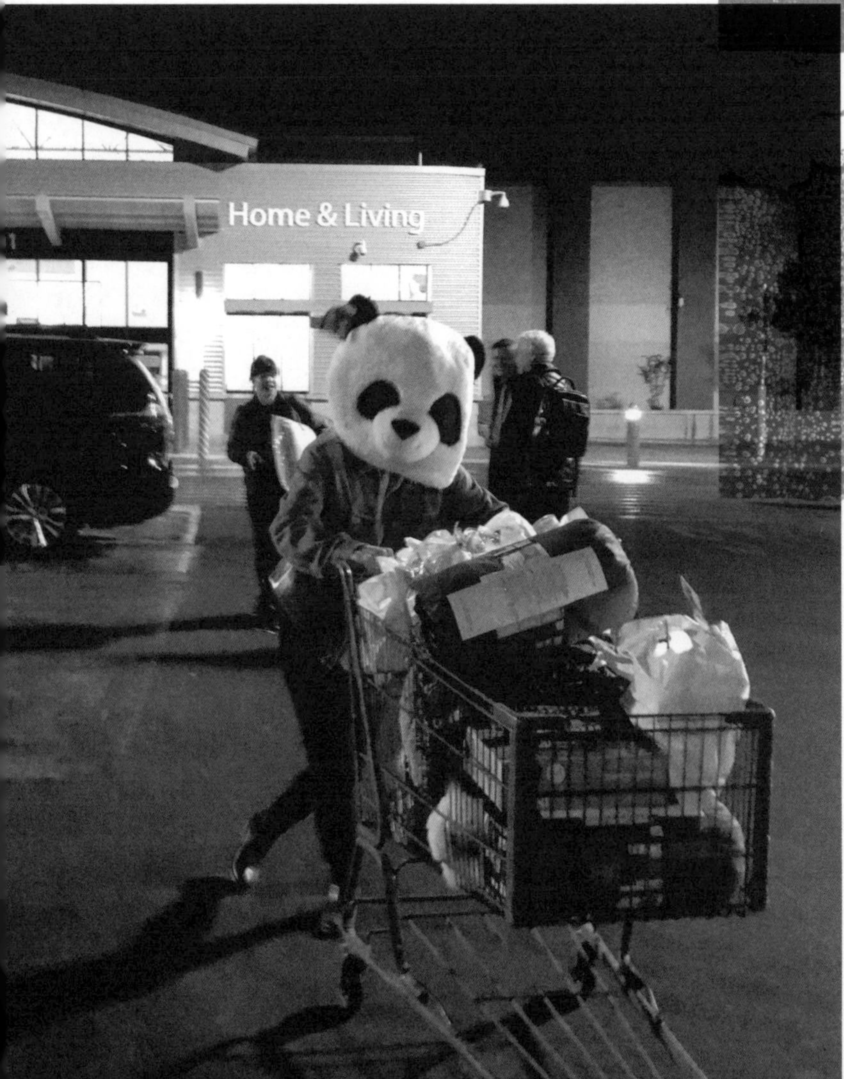
Home & Living

The Road:
Bakersfield II

Elections have consequences.
The people of Eastchester plant their flags.
What Bakersfield is and what it could be.
Questions from the Mayor.

F
F
T
T

-

11

-

18

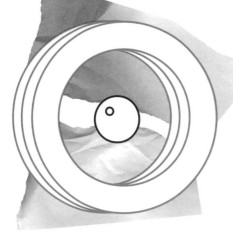

210

"One thing this town needs is infrastructure," Verda says after the jolt.

Everyone is riding in Paulina's car en route to dinner with Daniel Cater and his wife Monica at their home in the Westchester section of Bakersfield. Paulina has just slammed on the brakes to avoid hitting a man who steps out of the darkness on a block with no street lights. Suddenly, he's just *there* in her headlights...

"Oh my God!"

Nervous laughter at the close call and the narrowly averted dark turn to Food for Thought Truck's story: VISITING DESIGNERS KILL LOCAL MAN. Street lights, cross-walks—for a city of nearly 400,000 there's a noticeable paucity of urban structure in Bakersfield. It's as if the small-town mindset that survives from the period when Bakersfield *was* a small town (and probably accounts for all those warm interactions at Café Smitten yesterday) hasn't kept pace with the city's growth.

The issue comes up again at dinner. It is less than a week after the 2018 national elections and one of Daniel's and Monica's guests this evening is Bakersfield City Councilman Andrae Gonzales, who represents the district that encompasses Eastchester. Councilman Gonzales is coming off the bitter loss of a bond measure he supported that would have addressed some of those infrastructure issues. Measure N would have raised the local sales tax by 1 percent, with the money earmarked for public safety, homeless programs and yes, infrastructure —improvements to the city that would facilitate the high hopes everyone has for Eastchester. On election night Measure N came up short by about 2,000 votes. "It was heartbreaking," Gonzales says, "but after I cried myself to sleep a few nights, I realized, hey, 49 percent of people in this city voted to raise their own taxes to make this a better place. That's significant." Tonight the Councilman still has hopes that uncounted absentee ballots might push the measure over the finish line. All during dinner he checks his cell phone for updated totals.

The Bakersfield Californian

Vol. 91 • No. 354   BAKERSFIELD, CALIF., TUESDAY,   68 PAGES   6 SECTIONS   15¢

VISITING DESIGNERS KILL LOCAL MAN

(and are never invited back again)

Gale-force winds — with gusts to 50 and 60 miles per hour — whipped the southern San Joaquin Valley last night and today, leaving a trail of destruction.

The storm was kicked up by strong Santa Ana winds, the National Weather Service said. A large pressure differential between a storm system offshore and a strong high-pressure ridge over the Rocky Mountains caused the winds, weather officials said.

The wind's strength was said to be lighter in north Kern County-south Tulare County and was minimal in valley areas farther north. The Fresno area had zero visibility during the night from fog.

Interstate 5 was closed this morning from Laval Road to Grapevine, with traffic being turned back, the California Highway Patrol reported. And Highway 58 was closed this morning from Edison to Tehachapi.

KUZZ radio was off the air this morning; several schools closed, and some school districts delayed

opening two hours because of a combination of the wind and power outages caused by the wind.

Gusts up to 180 mph were reported in the Arvin area, with the highest recorded figure at Meadows Field National Weather Service station 47 mph at 3:47 this morning.

The winds were head on to planes at Meadows Field and the commercial aircraft "can handle that wind," a control tower spokesman said. But visibility was below the minimum for commercial crafts to land.

"They can depart but not land," he said at 7:45 a.m. "Visibility, because of the dust, is the problem, not the wind itself. The wind is 30 mph and they (the commercial craft) can handle that wind."

Power outages were reported all over the valley portion of the county, a Pacific Gas and Electric Co. spokesman said.

"Outage reports started coming in at 2 a.m. and have grown and grown since," he said. "As of 6

a.m. all crews were in the field where lines are reported down.

"About 7 a.m. more customers were out than in service to both the Bakersfield area and other valley areas. From Lebec to Arvin to the southern portion of Bakersfield was the most seriously affected areas as of 8 a.m."

Elevators and telephones were not operating at Kern County Administration and Courts Building this morning, due to the storm.

The CHP issued traffic advisories for the valley and recommended that campers and vehicles with trailers not travel. Highway 58 was closed about 7 a.m. and I-5 about the same time.

The CHP was turning southbound traffic back to Bakersfield at Laval Road — where I-5 and Highway 99 merge — and the Tejon CHP station was stopping northbound traffic at the Grapevine.

Several minor traffic accidents were reported due to wind but as of 8 a.m. there were no reports of

major wind-caused crashes, the CHP reported.

Several fires were reported and power lines were blown down, causing a rash of rescue calls for Bakersfield and county firemen.

The strong southeast winds are expected to continue tonight, the weatherman said, averaging 30 to 40 mph and gusting to 50 to 60. There will be increasing cloudiness today.

It will be mostly cloudy and continued mild tonight, then cloudy with a 50 percent chance of rain by late tomorrow. Winds will be lighter.

Yesterday's high in Bakersfield was 69 and last night's low 42. The winds will cause today's high to jump to 79, with an overnight low of 56 and a high tomorrow of 65 expected, the weatherman said.

Plane owners were advised yesterday of the approaching storm and all craft were secured, so there were no problems this morning with toppling aircraft, said Faro

see Storm — page 1

Staff photos by Jack Knight

...i High School, bucks high winds ...office this morning.

...winds rip ...rrible'

...ave Market, Bear ...levard and North A ...the roof was ripped ...sort of disintegrated." ...said the highest ...

'Fallen tree outside ... makes things ki...

Wind...
...ection of refuse

Most Kern County refuse collectors suspended operations today due to the high winds, according to Ken Renwick of the county Health Department.

Attempts to dump trash from bins and cans into trucks caused discarded papers and other refuse to be picked up by the howling wind, Renwick said.

"It was fruitless to continue," said John Varner, president of the Rubbish Disposal Association of Kern County.

Refuse operators said they will resume operations after the storm, picking up on regularly scheduled days. Tuesday's pickups, therefore, will not be made until Friday, the next regular pick-up day.

...ure operatio... ...Water Stora... ...cials reported

"It's terrib... before how to... Schnell, Arvi... her dispatcher... the size of po...

He said he... when the pow... eries could be...

And the A... ment reported... to several ar... according to... head dispatch...

This is the way it looked shortly after dawn this morning on Union Avenue at Brundage

...Lane. Visibility was minimal due to dust — not fog, for a change — blown by high winds.

Pilots say dust like A-bomb cloud

"It looked like someone dropped an a-bomb on Bakersfield," said Dick Powers, chief pilot for Continental Telephone Co., describing the view of the southern San Joaquin Valley from an airplane this morning.

Powers flew a company airplane from Meadows Field to Apple Valley this morning and had to climb to 6,000 feet to get over the dust from the Arvin-Lamont area,

He talked to a United Airlines pilot flying from San Francisco to Los Angeles who suggested the A-bomb comparison, a view Powers seconded.

The dust starts in the foothills beyond Edison with dirt peeling off the hills at about 2,000 feet.

"Porterville has zero-zero visibility with fog and is dead calm," Powers said. "There is just a strip across the top of us."

Another pilot told Powers he could see the airport at Taft when he flew over but from there north it was total oblivion.

"If you wear contact lenses you are in trouble outside," Powers said.

Desert weather is pleasant, he said. There are 10 to 15-knot winds from the north with no blowing dust apparent. It was choppy flying over the mountains

YOU HAVE ONLY 5 DAYS TO DO CHRISTMAS SHOPPING

In cities where infrastructure does not keep up with growth the potential for catastrophe increases with every failed tax measure.

F
F
T
T

-

11

-

18

It's a convivial evening. Because designers tend to design their lives more deliberately than other people, when a group of them gets together everything acquires a heightened awareness. Daniel and Monica's home feels welcoming in just the right way; tasteful, but unfussy. The Basque stew they serve isn't only delicious; it looks photographable bubbling on the stove. And designers talking shop is always a mix of strongly held views—"Did you see those shoes? My God!"—and casually dropped erudition:

"What's Ronchamp?" Al (a non-designer) asks after several mentions of Le Corbusier's landmark chapel.

Daniel smiles: "Al, that's one of those things you're supposed to pretend you know when it comes up in conversation."

Tonight feels energized by the events of the last two days. The Food for Thought Truck team is excited about how well the project is going and Daniel seems happy with the way the community has stepped up to participate. Austin Smith from the Pecha Kucha and his wife Anna who writes for *The Bakersfield Californian* are there with their toddler Teddy, and after a brief appearance by Daniel and Monica's baby Simone, the convergence of family and new friends seems almost perfectly designed.

Suddenly in the midst of the laughter and talk Andrae Gonzales makes the sound of a man who has badly stubbed his toe. Actually, it's his hopes that have banged a hard corner. The late count has just come in and Measure N is still over a thousand votes short. To have worked so hard on something for which the need is so apparent, the cause so incontestably just and to have it fail by such a narrow margin—a thousand votes out of almost a hundred thousand cast—must be excruciating. Still, Councilman Gonzales is a political pro, and but for that first ouch, he accepts this defeat in the middle of a dinner party with aplomb. Of the people present perhaps only the locals understand the depth of his disappointment.

"It's a long game, Andrae," Daniel says. "We'll win it next time."

- - -

Over 40 people drew boundaries for Eastchester during Food for Thought Truck's Day One exercise, a level of participation that exceeded the team's most optimistic expectations. The consensus that emerged was that Bakersfield's hottest new neighborhood is a swath of the city pretty much in alignment with what Daniel Cater has been at pains to show his guests.

Now on Days Two, Three and Four the "Imagine Eastchester" public visioning exercise turns to what should fall within those boundaries.

"Where's 20th please?" says a man peering at a new map of downtown mounted on the side of the truck. Verda shows him where 20th Street is, and he plants a little flag there with his idea for Eastchester printed on it. His wife leans in to look.

"Would you like to pin one?" Verda asks.

"Let me give it some thought," the woman says. "Actually, he's the one who's interested."

Her husband has pinned a flag for a new business venture he has in mind, something to do with financial planning. These two are examples of Bakersfield's retired community, but it's telling that they are just as interested—well, he is anyway—in the future of Eastchester as the city's young entrepreneurs. Through the week interested parties, young and old, fill up the map with tiny battle flags for what they want to see in this neighborhood. Five people pin up a food store—one stickler specifically a Whole Foods store. Three people pin a bookstore and three a music venue. The beer garden is there—presumably from the guy who drew it into his boundary map on Day One. And there are one-off flags for a variety of amenities: an art movie theater, a baker's outlet, a dog park, a card shop. The preponderance of flags is for these kinds of pleasure assets, but a few community-minded folk pin social improvement ideas: a recycling center, a pet rescue facility, a kids' art center, an African American/Latino Cultural Center… "Or maybe one for each," someone comments.

"It's sort of cool that things aren't set in stone here," a woman looking over the thicket of flag pins says. "For the past few years things have been happening in Bakersfield. Younger people are starting businesses. You can come from somewhere and you don't have to have a ton of money to live here. I mean: go to San Francisco and try to start something—when you're a young person?" She grimaces at the unlikeliness of that dream. "I like that things can happen here. It's not all locked down."

Precisely! As the week progresses it becomes increasingly clear to the Food for Thought Truck team that their role in Bakersfield is to provide a lightning rod for the community's creative electricity, a single locale where, for one week, focused bolts of inspiration and aspiration can land. When a few days into the project agents from the Bakersfield health

As the week progresses it becomes increasingly clear to the Food for Thought Truck team that their role in Bakersfield is to provide a lightning rod for the community's creative electricity, a single locale where, for one week, focused bolts of inspiration and aspiration can land.

department turn up to see if the truck has a permit for operating a food business, Verda explains it's not food they're peddling, it's food for *thought*.

- - -

Yes, but from the beginning she wanted the truck to be a workshop. She wanted to build stuff. Verda has already engaged a carpenter in Bakersfield to build the prototype of a public bench and planter combo she designed before the team left San Francisco. Ash Dipert knocked out the first components of the unit with a swiftness that left Fremont's mini-golf carpentry in the dust. He will be back on Thursday to put it all together at a public build in the parking lot.

In the meantime the team's other big physical project gets underway. On Saturday Lauren and Alex lay down a grid of chalk lines across a large section of pavement in front of Café Smitten. Using a chalked string technique that dates back to ancient Egypt they quickly snap a grid of 12 inch by 12 inch squares on the concrete. Into these squares the team will spray-stencil patterns that Paulina designed to represent Bakersfield: houses, water towers, stalks of wheat, circles and squares, rainbow arches, flower petals, abstract people. Paulina runs a couple of tests on Saturday, but the real work begins on the following day.

The first decision to be made is how to orient the mural on the pavement. In design, 'Which way is up?' is a question for which there is not always an obvious answer. It's a choice—and given the size of this piece and the fact that it will remain on the pavement

for two years or so until the parking lot becomes a housing development, it's not a trivial choice.

"I think the houses and the water towers should always read up," Alex says. "Those are the ones that are super-directional." But should they read up as you're coming into the café or as you're coming out? The team chooses to orient the piece to read up as you're entering—right side up the first time you see it, upside down on your way out.

Next thing to decide is the plan of attack. With over 200 squares to fill and only Sunday afternoon and Monday morning to fill them, there's no time for delay and no room for error.

"Who's done stenciling before?" Paulina asks.

In Banksy's film *Exit Through the Gift Shop* there's a great shot of a tagger blasting a long, swooping tail of paint on the side of a rapidly passing train. The image captures both the euphoria of transgressive art and the confidence required to make bold use of that instant when a spray of pigment hits its surface. Now outside of Café Smitten, with people watching from the outdoor tables, Food for Thought Truck's commando artists summon the confidence to tag their vision of Eastchester right on Eastchester's doorstep.

"I think the thing you want to do is use as little paint as possible," Verda explains by way of demonstration. "And you want to spray at one angle and then another angle because the lines become crisper." Verda has cut a square into a large piece of cardboard. She places this frame over one square of the pavement grid. Into the exposed concrete she drops a stencil of the wheat pattern and hits it with a blast of spray paint from two directions. When frame and stencil are lifted away, a crisp white image remains.

Thus instructed, the taggers begin. Uniformed in black pants, sneakers, Food for Thought Truck T-shirts and respiration masks Alex, Lauren, Paulina and Verda spread out and hit various sections of the grid. (Al, whose test square turned out a little mushy, gets the harmless job of cleaning off gunked-up stencils.)

And they bang it out. Once they get the rhythm, the Food for Thought Truckers rip through aerosol cans of paint like ecstatic graffiti masters on a multi-wall binge. Paulina's schematic located certain images in certain parts of the grid, but for the actual execution, what goes where is determined by the individual artist—no rules for taggers, dude! And as the giant pattern takes shape, the team determines that filling up all 200-plus squares would look cluttered.

This design needs to breathe. So they leave some areas of the pavement blank, giving the mural a lightness and playfulness that seems perfect for Café Smitten—and for Eastchester.

"It's getting too dark for me to see what I'm doing," Alex says.

Verda and Paulina get up extra early next morning to finish the job before Smitten opens and the smell of fresh paint puts people off their breakfast.

- - -

Food for Thought Truck structured the Bakersfield visit to be activity-heavy on the front and back end, but Bakersfield rocks every day of the week. Though part of the team returns to San Francisco on Monday and new members arrive later in the week, Verda and Al remain for the duration, and it is they who reap the benefits of Bakersfield's largesse.

David Coffey invites them to tour a house for sale, a mid-century gem not far from the Frank Lloyd Wright site. Perhaps Verda would like to move to Bakersfield? Shai and Stasie Bitton from Cafe Smitten welcome them at the groundbreaking for their next venture—an Italian-themed café in the Seven Oaks neighborhood. Perhaps they can come back next year for the grand opening? The Mayor of Bakersfield attends the groundbreaking, and Verda invites her to Food for Thought Truck's wrap party. Kern County officials ask Verda to come in and talk about possible branding projects for the public library and the county as a whole. Kristina Pirtle, a teacher at Christa McAuliffe Elementary, invites the team to come and speak to her class of fourth graders—a roomful of exuberant, brightly shining young daredevils. "Anyone want to drive the truck home for me?" Verda asks, and the 10-year-olds' hands all shoot up.

One afternoon Daniel takes Verda and Al on a tour of Bakersfield's east side—"East of Eastchester," he calls it. Verda drives while Daniel provides an extraordinary block-by-block commentary: "This is Luigi's. It's been in operation for a hundred years. There's a warehouse where they have gelato and a little Italian grocery store... Over that way there's a really good Mercado Latino and a plaza with mariachi and stuff... These little two-stories, they used to be hotels with restaurants below... This is the old train station—just waiting to be restored... This is the old vaudeville theater..." And on and on—it's an object lesson in how an architect inhabits a city. Where most people walk by an old building barely registering what

they pass, an architect walks by an example of his trade, a layer of his city's history, perhaps a step in the development of his own aesthetic.

The destination of this tour is David Nelson Park in East Bakersfield. Named for a local police officer killed in the line of duty, the 'pocket park' was designed by Daniel and developed by Andrae Gonzales's non-profit, Children First Campaign, in a part of town that Daniel describes as forgotten by the city. "There are parts that don't even have curbs and gutters and sidewalks," he says. Or stoplights. As they get out of the car to look at the park a woman pushing a shopping cart crosses a busy street in mid-block, warily navigating the traffic rushing by. The park is a modest expanse of green with a mural at one end painted by local artists as 'a love letter' to East Bakersfield.

Daniel unlocks the gate. (Because the sod for the green has just been put down, the park is closed until it seeds.) When the pocket park opens, he explains, it will be administered by the Pan Dulce Club, a group of mothers from Williams Elementary who are the unofficial stewards of the neighborhood. "Children First entrusted each of the moms with a key to the park," Daniel says. "Each one takes one day of the week and opens it at sunrise and closes it at sunset." It's the sort of partnership he envisions blossoming all over Bakersfield —communities pressing the city for change and then stepping up to manage the changes themselves. Out here in the sun, with the traffic rolling and the minimalist park unoccupied, it may seem a small step, but Daniel knows how far small steps can take you. ("It's a long game, Andrae.") Now that David Nelson Park exists, he says, the city is interested in developing two similar patches of land in 'forgotten' East Bakersfield. That lady with the shopping cart may get her stoplight yet.

- - -

If one person can be credited with authorship of the Bakersfield leg of Food for Thought Truck's journey it is Kristina Cho. At the first concept meeting her sketches of a possible week in Bakersfield laid out a program for the truck remarkably similar to the week now in progress at Café Smitten. As Daniel's friend and former work associate, she first brought O+A and Cater Design Group together. She served as liaison with Daniel through the course of the project. She worked with the team on activities and logistics. In its early phases, at least, this project was her baby. But when the time came actually to go to Bakersfield

FFTT

-
11
-
18

215

Esai Mendez is developing a yoga manual with exercises designed especially for field workers. He's been studying kinesiology to better understand the impact a full day of picking fruits and vegetables has on a person's back and neck.

F
F
T
T

-

11
-
18

ᴦ ᴦ ᴦ scheduling conflicts kept her from taking part. So there's a sense of a last piece falling into place when Kristina finally parachutes in on Wednesday night.

Keeping the truck staffed has been more of a challenge than anyone expected. A pro bono project's greatest expense is the time allotted to participating employees, and with O+A barely staffed to cover its commercial obligations, giving away billable hours has been painful. Still, the hit-and-miss staffing on Food for Thought Truck has created some weird disconnects. From a creative fulfillment perspective, it makes no sense to send Paulina, Alex and Lauren on the road to do all the heavy lifting in Bakersfield and then yank them back to the office before they can take part in the community's celebration of their work.

Project interruptus!

And it doesn't feel right that the Food for Thought Truckers most responsible for getting the thing up and running in its early stages—George, Chase, Kristina, Nikki, Marbel—are not on hand for at least one stage of the journey when the truck hits the road. Okay, Nikki has moved on and Marbel has been away on maternity leave, but what about the others? Kristina's late arrival in Bakersfield allows her to touch the project she conceived before it quite wraps up, but though she remains characteristically circumspect on the matter, it seems a miserly allowance of time given what a success her Bakersfield project is turning out to be.

- - -
Esai Mendez is developing a yoga manual with exercises designed especially for field workers. He's been studying kinesiology to better understand the impact a full day of picking fruits and vegetables has on a person's back and neck. He consulted with a friend who is a yoga instructor to devise a program specifically addressing the appropriate pressure points. His manual will be a downloadable teaching guide for yoga instructors offering special classes to farm workers. It's a dizzying mix of science, art, yoga, book design, social justice, physical therapy: "I'm putting all of the aspects of my life together into one," Esai explains.

"That's what I'm trying to do," Verda says.

Nicole Grisso is studying the health impact of oil jack pumps on children. "You guys aren't from Bakersfield," she says, "but there are a lot of oil jack pumps on school grounds here. My project is around all the respiratory issues we have with pollution and how they affect the kids directly." She's creating an activity book to alert parents and children to those issues.

"So the idea is they research this thing," Bill Kelley Jr. says. "They go find people in the community they can talk to about it and from that they develop a proposal for the project." Kelley is Assistant Professor of Latin American and Latino Art at California State University in Bakersfield (CSUB) and a strong advocate for art as a vehicle for social change. He has brought his class,

Esai and Nicole among them, to see this literal vehicle dedicated to a similar aesthetic.

"I didn't find out about this until Tuesday," Kelley says. He had stopped by Café Smitten, noticed the truck in the parking lot and tapped on its window. "Part of the dynamic I'm realizing, just having moved here from LA," he says, "is that the university seems to be kind of..." He searches for the right word: "... isolated? From the rest of the city. I think it's a condition of Bakersfield in general. It's slightly segregated."

Verda is riffing on what might have been. "I would love to have collaborated with you on a project. I would definitely like to take this toward a more charged discussion than just, 'How can we make your community more beautiful?'" She describes Food for Thought Truck's upcoming partnership with River LA and mentions how it was inspired by a Chicana artist known for erecting unauthorized plaques to document LA's 'erased histories.'

"Sandra de la Loza," Bill Kelley says. "I'm inviting her to come and speak next semester."

Verda winces with the pain of missed opportunity. "Oh, I wish I was around!"

– – –

On Friday evening people gather at Café Smitten to say goodbye to Food for Thought Truck. Children hopscotch across the pavement art—an unanticipated use that now seems obvious. Guests nibble finger food catered by the café and take pictures sitting in the bench/planter Ash completed yesterday. A loop of photographs of the week's interactions cycles across the old Pecha Kucha screen. It's a measure of the warmth of the city's welcome that the folks in attendance this evening are already familiar faces. The project's stalwarts are present—Daniel Cater and David Coffey, Ariel Dyer and Anna Smith, but so are people who merely stopped by the truck once or twice on their way to coffee. So are 'the regulars' who visited the truck almost daily to pick up the 'Imagine Eastchester' conversation where it left off the day before.

As the sun goes down and a cool breeze rises, Verda thanks them all. It's a low-key farewell, the sort of thank-you you would give a friend after a dinner party, knowing that this goodbye is but a pause, these good times ongoing, this friendship destined to continue.

The Mayor's visit caps the evening. When earlier in the week Mayor Karen Goh said she'd come to the wrap party everyone from Food for Thought Truck assumed a quick politician's visit to shake some hands,

take some selfies and then move on to the next group of voters. Mayor Goh not only makes the rounds; she chats at length with members of the team, climbs into the truck and grills them on what they have learned. She's interested in their impressions of Bakersfield, but most of all she wants to know what Bakersfield's citizens had to say about their city. She wants to know what her constituents have on their minds. In the hubbub of the wrap party it's not clear that anything the Food for Thought Truckers report is of any practical use to the Mayor, but afterwards when the team have had time to reflect on their week, the relevant themes, practical and otherwise, emerge.

F
F
T
T

–

11

F
F
T
T

-

11
-
18

218

F
F
T
T
-
11
-
18

220

F
F
T
T

-

11

-

18

222

Bakersfield and Food for Thought Truck told each other the same story—their messages, it turned out, were perfectly in sync: keep going, keep innovating, don't be discouraged by setbacks or disappointments. Reality resists improvement, sure, but the right coalition can overcome resistance.

F
F
T
T

11

18

r r r What did the people of Bakersfield tell Food for Thought Truck about their city?

They said through words and actions that they loved their stretch of sunshine two hours north of LA—loved that it wasn't LA and weren't looking for it to become that mega-city's northernmost suburb. They wanted Bakersfield emphatically to remain what it is, but the best version possible of what it is. They valued the friendliness of their city and the small-town roots from which it sprang.

224 They valued it enough to come home to Bakersfield after trying out alternative lives in places like Los Angeles and San Francisco and New York—and even Copenhagen. And they viewed coming home not as a retreat from the larger world, but as another adventure, applying what they learned outside to their native contexts. They said they wanted some help with that project in the form of open minds from their fellow citizens and open arms from their city and county governments. They conceded that Bakersfield needed a haircut, needed a shave— streetlights and crosswalks, new energy in places that had too long been dormant: grocery stores and bookstores, an arts center maybe, a recycling center maybe and, okay, a beer garden. They said they wanted a closer link between the city and its university, CSUB. All that talent simmering in those classrooms, all that opportunity out there

in the general populace—why segregate those natural allies? And they said most forcefully that they were eager to be part of making a new Bakersfield—that they had ideas and dreams for the city that were personal and public at the same time. They appreciated the lightning rod, but they wanted this storm of creativity and forward thinking to rumble in Bakersfield's big sky for years to come.

Bakersfield and Food for Thought Truck told each other the same story—their messages, it turned out, were perfectly in sync: keep going, keep innovating, don't be discouraged by setbacks or disappointments. Reality resists improvement, sure, but the right coalition can overcome resistance. A lot of people love what you're doing. Keep doing it. Keep rolling. You're on the right track.

- - -

A postscript: A couple of weeks after Food for Thought Truck returns to San Francisco, Daniel Cater emails good news. The late vote count for the 2018 election that decided several close Congressional races in California, flipping seats from Republican to Democratic hands (mail-in ballots, provisional ballots, that sort of thing)—that vote count in Bakersfield pushed Measure N to victory by 97 votes.

"Andrae keeps holding victory parties," Daniel says. "I told him, you only won by 97 votes. Maybe you should tone it down a bit."

But how could anyone with big plans for Bakersfield feel anything but elation? Now the city will have revenue to back up its champions, the activists and agitators like Daniel and Monica Cater, David Coffey, Shai and Stasie Bitton, Bill Kelley Jr., Anna and Austin Smith and all those people who pinned flags of hope to their self-defined map of Eastchester. Sure, 97 votes out of nearly a hundred thousand cast is hardly an overwhelming mandate. But as designers know, an inch one way or the other can make all the difference in whether a design works beautifully or has to be scrapped. Ariel Dyer— librarian, musician, philosopher of ethics and Pecha Kucha star—might frame it this way: Bakersfield will move forward because those 97 voters showed up.

F
F
T
T
-
11
-
18

229

F
F
T
T

-

11

-

18

.

The Road: Los Angeles

LA has a river?
The truck in transit.
Verda rides a rodeo bull.
Amy and Verda live outlaw dreams.

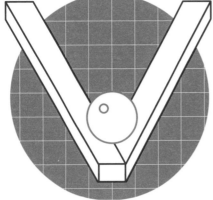

F
F
T
T
-
03
-
19

234

MARCH 2019

Verda and Al stop one morning at a Fedex in downtown LA to get copies made of a cardboard cutout of the Food for Thought Truck. It's an origami exercise that proved popular with young children in Bakersfield—you color the truck, cut it out and fold it into a little scale model. The team will be visiting high schools with River LA this week to help raise awareness of the Los Angeles River. High school kids are probably a little old for this kind of thing, but Verda wants to have a few cutouts on hand just in case—who knows what a budding designer or architect might make of them? Two men waiting in line look on patiently.

"That's a nice thing," one of them says. "Is that for kids?"

Al briefly explains the project with River LA.

"I didn't even know there was a river in LA," the second man says.

"That's exactly why we're here."

"I've seen it," the first man laughs. "That big concrete ditch, right? People use it for a dump. And taggers. They shoot movies there. *Fast and Furious*?"

"And *Grease*," Al says.

The second man shakes his head. "I've never seen a river in LA."

This conversation is taking place less than half a mile from the Los Angeles River.

- - -

When you fly over Los Angeles the city's river is dramatically visible, but if you don't know what you're looking at you might miss it. It is indeed a big concrete ditch and from the air looks more like a marvel of engineering than a feature of the natural landscape. It is both. In the 1930s the Army Corps of Engineers began the process of paving the river after floods destroyed homes and infrastructure in two separate events a mere four years apart. In retrospect paving the river seems an over-zealous solution to a periodic flooding problem, but in the 1930s LA's politics of growth and self-promotion could not abide the vagaries of nature. And unlike the Thames, say, or the Seine or the Hudson,

The LA River is where
Los Angeles began, but
a lot of people who
live near it, don't
know it exists.

F
F
T
T

—

03

—

19

the Los Angeles River was never a major natural waterway. In the arid climate of Southern California it was sometimes, and in some places, little more than a dried-up creek. One of the things that made its floods so devastating was that they seemed to come out of nowhere, not from a river with a substantial and consistent year-round presence.

Even so the LA River was as seminal to the development of its metropolis as those other rivers were to theirs. The Tongva Indians who first inhabited the Los Angeles Basin made their villages along the river, and the Spanish settlers who displaced (and enslaved) them built their pueblo in the same place. Twentieth-century LA famously turned elsewhere for its water supply, and the resulting giant effectively erased its birth river from public consciousness.

Twenty-first-century LA wants it back.

"The river is a 40- or 50-year project," says Jason Foster, Director of Strategic Partnerships at River LA. "That's why we focus on youth programming, because the young people are the people who will be able to see the finished product, and I think getting them bought in now is essential to them being champions of it later."

From an urban planning perspective, interest in the LA River is higher now than it has been at any time since the firm of Olmsted and Bartholomew proposed a network of parks and recreation spaces along its banks in 1930. The plan apparently horrified the business-minded Chamber of Commerce that commissioned it, and it was quietly shelved. Today's interest comes from people with Olmsted and Bartholomew's vision in mind, but also from commercial property developers, which is why any plan to 'restore' or 'revitalize' the river inevitably runs into controversy. Restore for whom? Revitalize what? In California, where housing prices are among the highest in the nation, issues of gentrification and community displacement confront every urban improvement project, however well-intentioned. River LA sees its mission as bringing all factions together on a river improvement program that benefits everybody. "I think there are endless doors that people can enter to really come in contact with our project," Jason Foster says. "What excites me is to try to make those doors."

So when Food for Thought Truck reached out to River LA, Jason Foster saw the possibility of another door. Over a period of weeks he and River

> River LA sees its mission as bringing all factions together on a river improvement program that benefits everybody. "I think there are endless doors that people can enter to really come in contact with our project," Jason Foster says. "What excites me is to try to make those doors."

LA CEO Angela Barranco worked with the truck's team to plan a wayfinding project that would address one of the chief obstacles to consensus development in river planning—the fact that a lot of Angelenos don't know the river exists.

- - -

For Food for Thought Truck, Los Angeles feels like a victory lap. Long months of uncertainty over what the truck was going to be, how it was going to work, if it was going to work, ended, once and for all, in Bakersfield. If the team's hidden fear was that the truck's real-world accomplishments—a one-day pocket park, a rejected display unit, a mini-golf attraction—would be too modest for its high-flying aspirations, the week of community visioning outside Café Smitten put that fear to rest. The depth of engagement in Bakersfield felt like a fulfillment of the team's highest hopes. To move on to Los Angeles seems a logical next step.

It is also an escalation. The sheer scale of River LA's itinerary for the project assures the truck a sweeping last effort. And because it will take place in different locations along the 51 miles of the river there is a satisfying sense of stitching communities together. The thread is the river, but the needle is a wayfinding sign designed by O+A graphic artist Amy Young: "You are X miles from the LA River." The plan is to place these signs, each with its distance custom printed, all over Los Angeles. In early planning for the project the team researched sites in Santa Monica (You are 17 miles from the LA River), Pasadena (12.6 miles), Echo Park (6.3 miles). There was even talk of

F
F
T
T

-

03
-
19

237

F
F
T
T
—
03
—
19

238

A successful project
is sweetest when
it's done. Amy (left)
designed the LA
River sign; Kristina
(right) conceived the
Bakersfield adventure.

rrr A ceaseless flow of traffic is the LA river everybody knows. To ease into that flow is to surrender to the ethos of a city forever in motion.

F
F
T
T
-

03
-
19

240

making signs for O+A's projects around the country —say, at McDonald's headquarters in Chicago (2,015 miles) or Nike's Digital Innovation Studio in Manhattan (2,797 miles).

Luckily Brandon Tate, the young River LA staffer filling in while Jason Foster is away on paternity leave, has compiled a list of schools and businesses in a more pragmatic sequence. "Really the focus that I had was using the river as a spine for the city," he says, "and trying to have locations that corresponded with the miles, the 51 miles."

On Monday morning Verda and Brandon head out with a truckload of signs.

It is Verda's first time driving the truck, and she isn't looking forward to it. "I'm just going to go slow, and I don't care if I get honked at," she says, unconvincingly. Pulling the truck out of River LA's parking lot in the Arts District, she is like a rodeo rider settling atop a new Brahma bull. Fortunately there's a distraction almost instantly. "Oh, here we are at the river!"

As it rolls across the 4th Street Bridge, Food for Thought Truck gets its first close look at what it has come to celebrate. On the one hand it's an image of industrial blight so perfect it's almost beautiful: a flat, straight, paved channel with sloping concrete embankments, railroad tracks and power lines on either side. On the other hand, even as it flashes by, the hidden force of nature beneath the pavement comes through strongly. You can imagine the river as a Hollywood superhero encased in hard restraints by the Army Corps of Engineers finally cracking its straitjacket and shaking off chunks of concrete— all this recreated in slow motion IMAX CGI and Premium Dolby sound.

"Just to let you know the pavement will get a little shoddy as we get close to the freeway," Brandon warns. No sooner has he spoken than the

rodeo bull begins to buck and jump. Verda holds on tight through a wild ride, objecting with profane emphasis to every teeth-rattling jolt. A moment later, however, when she is sliding from the on-ramp onto 101 North, some fundamental threshold of resistance seems to have passed. The travel writer Jan Morris once wrote of this sensation—this moment of merging into traffic on an LA freeway. A ceaseless flow of traffic is the LA river everybody knows. To ease into that flow is to surrender to the ethos of a city forever in motion.

"I'm on the freeway!" Verda cries, and Food for Thought Truck cruises north to Canoga Park.

"Where are we going to put those?" Curtis Ward says to his visitors.

"We were going to leave that up to you. Maybe on the lawn here?" Brandon poses a yard sign where it might go.

"The problem with yard signs—you know what's going to happen. These are high school kids." Curtis Ward is the Careers Magnet Coordinator at Canoga Park High, and he wears the can't-be-rattled expression of a middle-aged man who spends his day with teenagers. Verda and Brandon have arrived with a full array of window stickers, posters and yard signs. Ward likes the metal landmark sign better than the yard version and wants to make sure it is placed where it will be safe from mischief and its message will be accurate. "We've got a tributary over there," he says, "and a tributary over there, and they come together right behind the football field." The confluence of Bell Creek and Arroyo Calabasas is generally agreed to be the beginning of the Los Angeles River, and Brandon has chosen it as the place to kick off the sign placement project. He calculated the distance from the front of the school, and Curtis Ward agrees the metal gate that secures the entrance is the perfect spot to remind arriving students, faculty and staff each morning, "You are 1056 feet from the LA River."

"I'll have Carlos put that up," he says.

Over the next three days Food for Thought Truck and River LA hit locations around the city, some chosen by Brandon, some by Verda; some are close to the river, some miles away. In between stops they sail along the freeway. Of all the Food for Thought Truck projects this one is the purest road trip, the one that makes best use of the truck as a truck.

Its stops have the episodic quality of a Kerouac novel. At MASH Studios in Culver City (You are 5.7 miles from the LA River), Bernard Brucha brings his whole staff outside for an impromptu presentation by Verda. Bernard has been a friend of O+A for years and MASH is a close partner, making custom furniture for big commercial projects. Bernard's studio is itself an example of the transformative power of design. A run-down warehouse in a sketchy part of town when MASH moved in, it is now an elegant workshop where beautiful objects are made. At Clara Park in Cudahy (You are 0.55 miles from the LA River), mariachi music plays in the senior center as elderly celebrants arrive for a midday fiesta. Brandon and Verda put up a yard sign on the lawn and drop off truck cutouts and a landmark sign inside. The cheery lady at the reception desk gratefully accepts the cutouts "para los niños" and promises to have her manager install the landmark sign. Her goodbye overflows with "gracias."

At the Vitra showroom in another part of Culver City (You are 9.1 miles from the LA River), the sign goes up right inside the store. Verda meets Edie Cohen there, West Coast Editor of *Interior Design Magazine* and they pose for pictures inside the truck like LA school girls. At Spoke Bicycle Café in Frogtown (You are 215 feet from the LA River), a door opens in the fence that surrounds the alfresco dining area, and there's the river! It looks more like a traditional river here than at 4th Street: a stony shoreline, some tenacious plant life, not much water on this day, but frogs, probably, if you venture down to the rocks. Surely there are frogs in Frogtown. At Palos Verdes High School in Palos Verdes (You are 12.3 miles from the LA River), art students form a semi-circle around the truck while Verda pitches O+A and Brandon pitches River LA. The truck cutouts from Fedex are a big hit here—artists of any age can make magic with cardboard and color.

"I want to buy this truck!" their teacher says as her students swarm inside.

In the end there isn't time to make all the stops on Brandon's ambitious list. No day is ever long enough for LA's boundless scale. But if Brandon will still have signs to deliver after Food for Thought Truck goes home, there is a sense of seeds sown for the future as this phase of the project winds down.

On the last day of the visit, Verda and Amy (who has come down at the end to see her handiwork in action) set out on foot to pepper the Arts District with Food for Thought Truck stickers and to slap up unauthorized posters under some pre-scouted construction scaffolding. "Add tickets and bail to the budget," Lisa had said in an early meeting, and from that day Food for Thought Truck fancied itself an outlaw operation. All through the journey the project has simmered with an unfulfilled urge to build something and install it without permission —to swoop into a community overnight and leave behind a structure like 3D taggers. Now, in LA, that outlaw impulse finally breaks loose—well, sort of. "Excuse me," random passersby smile as they edge

03
-
19

241

"Add tickets and bail to the budget," Lisa had said in an early meeting, and from that day Food for Thought Truck fancied itself an outlaw operation. All through the journey the project has simmered with an unfulfilled urge to build something and install it without permission...

one continuous body passing through communities that collectively make up Los Angeles. Maybe up here above those factions really is the best point from which to measure—both the distance to the river and the distance to its eventual fate. Asked to describe how they hope to spend a day on the river 50 years from now, the two young men from River LA answer thoughtfully.

Brandon says, "I want to see the river as an attraction, something that represents Los Angeles as an iconic symbol of the city. I would like to see murals or maybe even statues."

"My vision is much more homely," Jason says. "Being able to drive east from where I live now in South Central, pop right over to Southgate, Compton, Bell. I'd like to enter the park, grab a coffee and be able to sit there and just chill. That is ultimately what I look forward to." After a pause he adds, "And hopefully I won't be the only person there."

politely past the renegade wheatpasters. With posters, brushes and pails of glue, Verda and Amy for a few delicious moments live the lawless life of Food for Thought Truck's dreams. When they have slathered enough glue on a lineup of posters to create a wall of river wayfinding, they stop to pose for pictures like real outlaws eager to claim their crimes.

The final lawful sign goes up a short distance away at Shimoda Design Group. Contract Magazine named Joey Shimoda Designer of the Year in 2013, two years after Verda and Primo received the honor. They have been good friends ever since. Now out on Joey Shimoda's balcony, Verda and Amy wire in place the day's last sign 10 or 15 feet off the ground: "You are 0.3 miles from the LA River." High in the air seems an appropriate place for Food for Thought Truck's last stop. The project began over a year ago well off the ground in conceptual terms and through the months of its bumpy progress was again and again pulled back to earth. Now, after the successes of Bakersfield and LA, it returns to its natural elevation. It's so in keeping with Paulina's fanciful graphics that the truck in the end should simply take wing.

Appropriate, too, perhaps for the LA River. Rising above the factions that struggle over this city's future, it is clear from the air that the river is

243

244

246

F
F
T
T

-

03

-

19

250

251

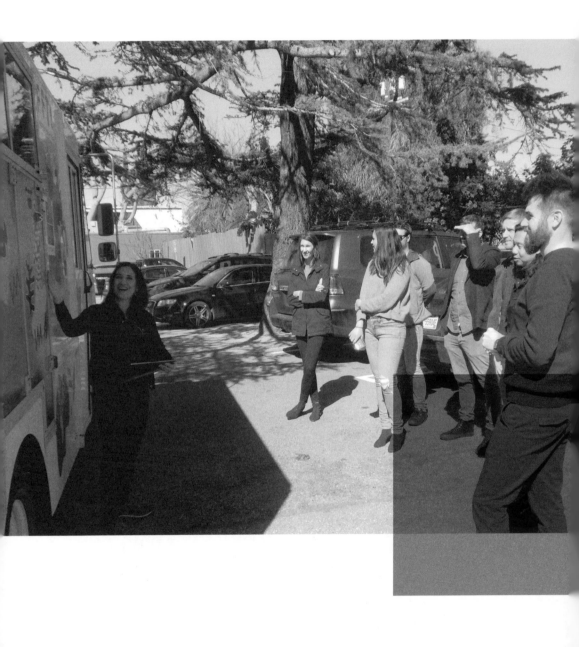

F
F
T
T

-

03
-
19

Epilogue

Was it worth it?
Was it fun?
Did it all work out?
Looking ahead to Season 2.

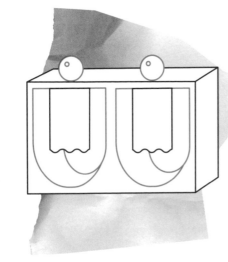

MAY 2019

"Where are you going next?"

It is the question that follows Food for Thought Truck everywhere. Where in the sense of itinerary, but also where in design terms, where in your aspirations? From the beginning the truck was a vehicle of two kinds. On the move it was a rattling, windy contraption, only marginally roadworthy. That it made it to Bakersfield and back, to Los Angeles and back, without incident, was considered a blessing by everyone who drove it. "What is that weird sound?" Verda asked the first time she took the wheel in LA. A rhythmic thumping had begun that persisted in Los Angeles and all the way back to San Francisco.

A rhythmic thumping attended, too, the creative thinking behind the truck's projects. Food for Thought Truck was never a carefully planned, exquisitely executed series of design interventions. It was always bigger, wilder, more ambitious in the brainstorming sessions at O+A than out on the road where reality tended to scale things back.

Some of this had to do with money. The upfront costs of Food for Thought Truck—buying the truck, getting it fitted out, getting it tuned up and ready to roll, plus the individual project expenses—sod for PARK(ing) Day, materials to build the golf hole, etc.—represented a significant pro-bono outlay for O+A even before the main expense of staff time was factored in. As a result there were never enough non-billable hours available to do the job 'properly'—whatever the job might be.

As its trips unfolded, what Verda consistently called the truck's 'scrappy' quality came to be recognized as an asset. Though a departure from O+A's typical design focus, Food for Thought Truck was, like so much of the firm's best work, an example of what it sought to do. Each project—from the rolling park, complete with bird sounds, to the river sign wired on Joey Shimoda's balcony—was an improvisation, an experiment on the impact design could have on non-design contexts. Starting with the ice cream truck it never got to be, Food for Thought Truck brought to unlikely venues—an abandoned

With their first
season done, the
Food for Thought
Truck team feels
they're ready finally
to tackle the
project properly.

"As far as leading the charge with something pretty radical and pretty different I think the Food Truck really fit the bill there. I'm really happy with it from that perspective."

shopping center, a forgotten neighborhood, an unloved river—the empathy of an attentive eye. That it rolled into town in funky, circus-wagon style surely made its partnerships more meaningful. Had it been sleekly designed, better equipped, more corporate, it's unlikely the good people of Eastchester would have returned day after day to pick up conversations begun the night before. Had it exuded money and a firm agenda, it could not have been as easily a guest of its hosts. Food for Thought Truck fit right in wherever it traveled. The process of unfolding the truck, screwing on its legs, lowering its platform acquired over time for those who repeated it the satisfaction of a nomad's ritual. Pitch the tent! Make camp here! George and Nikki's programming concept ultimately proved spot on—to be effective chuck everything out the window and hit the road with bare essentials and your wealth of ideas.

So… "Where are you going next?"

At the time of this writing, Verda sees two possible futures for the truck. The first and in some ways most attractive—for who does not dream, once embarked on a course of action, of taking another path?—is to sell the truck. In talking to people all over the world she has never encountered anyone who didn't think Food for Thought Truck was a wonderful idea. Within the design world people figuratively slap their foreheads that they didn't think of it themselves. Finding a buyer presumably would not be difficult.

But that slap on the forehead suggests another way forward—and a next life more in keeping with Food for Thought Truck's first. "I just feel like it could really be a great way to get design firms to team up and work together," Verda says. Her notion

is to make Food for Thought Truck a nonprofit foundation funded by grants. "So the idea would be other design firms would submit proposals and the Food for Thought Truck coordinator would plan the trip. I was thinking of a collaboration between myself and O+A and these other firms." The special appeal of this plan is that it spreads the expense across three separate entities—Food for Thought Truck Foundation, Studio O+A and the host firm. More importantly from a conceptual perspective, it represents a non-competitive alliance among design firms and a not-for-profit alliance between these firms and the community—not just 'good design,' but 'good for the planet, good for the culture, good for society design.' There's a growing awareness that the world today's successful people are leaving for their children (and everyone else's) is not necessarily one to be proud of. The imperative to create sustainable systems of cooperation and coordination looks more and more urgent in an increasingly fractious age. Turning business competitors into partners for a greater good would be a step in that direction.

On a sunny spring day at O+A's office in San Francisco, Verda grows visibly animated at the thought. "Now that we've got some trips under our belt and we've learned a lot about how to coordinate these stops and how to use our resources, I have confidence that we could do more impactful projects. Bakersfield, for example: I loved the fact that it was a combination of thinking, design thinking and planning and something tangible that we left behind. And so going forward I would definitely want to be more tactical, more strategic in what stops we choose." Outside in the parking lot, Food for Thought Truck, awaits its next assignment. "As far as leading the charge with something pretty radical and pretty different I think the Food Truck really fit the bill there. I'm really happy with it from that perspective. I think the day-to-day logistics and what actually happened and all of that is just what it is. It would definitely be good to sit down and think about what's next." She laughs—that signature Verda Alexander laugh: part surprise, part self-mockery, part awareness that the real world is never entirely anticipated in the drawings. "I think I haven't been taking this as seriously as I should."

Photography Credits

Color Photography

Elexa Henderson

Black and White Photography

Aditi Saldanha

Al McKee

Alex Pokas

Amy Young

Brandon Tate

Javier Gallardo

Lisa Bieringer

Lauren Harrison

Paulina McFarland

Verda Alexander

Cover Design

Hamda Al Naimi

Paulina McFarland

Verda Alexander / Artist

Verda Alexander's fine art perspective at Studio
O+A has spurred innovation and challenged received
wisdom throughout the design industry. Expanding the
dialogue between art and design, she has directed
her most recent efforts to the future of work
and exploring the impact design has on lives.
In 2018 Verda launched a small studio within O+A
to work exclusively on experimental projects and
unconventional interventions. That studio's first
project was Food For Thought Truck. While Verda
considers the truck's Phase 2, she is working on
a project with Love Good Color, an art commission
in Seattle, and a drawing class for designers.
Her appetite for stirring things up remains unabated.

Elizabeth Vereker / Design Director

Elizabeth Vereker is Design Director at Studio
O+A. As art director and designer of four books
for the company, she has employed her expertise in
interiors, design strategy, branding and graphic
design to create an enduring record of the firm's
evolution. A committed bibliophile and lover of
typography, Elizabeth uses precise systems design
techniques to arrive at graphics that seem to spring
from organic sources. Drawing inspiration from her
four-footed design consultant Ruby, Elizabeth looks
forward to her next appointment with a blank grid.

Al McKee / Writer

As Head Writer at Studio O+A, Al McKee has written
five books that explore the challenges, nuances and
social implications of workplace design. His work has
appeared in The New York Times, Metropolis, Threepenny
Review, Film Quarterly, Film Comment, Scenario and
Zyzzyva. He is the author of three unpublished novels
and remains hopeful of one day seeing them in print.

Paulina McFarland / Designer

As a Senior Brand Designer at Studio O+A she is known
for her highly creative graphics, witty illustrations
and concepts that challenge conventional values.
As creative director of the Oakland-based Aorta Art
Collective, she published Aorta Magazine, which
featured emerging feminist, queer and transgender
artists. Her work has appeared in Metropolis and
Interior Design Magazine and now includes product
and textile design. This is her first book. It won't
be her last.

Studio O+A

Design Direction
Verda Alexander & Elizabeth Vereker

Graphic Design & Illustration
Paulina McFarland

Author
Al McKee

Editor
Justin Lewis

Artifice Press Limited
81 Rivington Street,
London EC2A 3AY
United Kingdom
+44 (0)20 8371 4047
office@artificeonline.com
www.artificeonline.com

All opinions expressed within this
publication are those of the authors
and not necessarily of the publisher.

British Library in Cataloguing Data
A CIP record for this book is available
from the British Library

ISBN 978-1-911339-24-3

Printed by CPi Colour, London.